Dear Stephanie,

REAL WEALTH

Creating the Life You Deserve...
From the Inside Out

With love,

Phil Smedstad

REAL WEALTH

Creating the Life You Deserve...
From the Inside Out

by Phillip Smedstad

How to experience inner and outer abundance by transforming your life from fear-based to love-filled

**Theophilus Publications
Minneapolis, MN**

This book is based on my experience of the teachings of Jesus, as found in both *The Gospels* and in *A Course In Miracles*. The ideas expressed within are my interpretation of the concepts found in both of these resources.

A Course In Miracles was retypeset in 1992. This retypesetting included the numbering of all sections, paragraphs and sentences. The quotes I use from *The Course* are identified by the page number from this second edition.

Printed in the United States of America.
Cover design by Jan Joseph
Text layout by John Donaghy

ISBN 1-883044-04-9

For information, write:
The Rev. Phillip Smedstad
Theophilus Divinity School
3018 East Lake Street
Minneapolis, MN 55406

Acknowledgments

There are many people I want to acknowledge for their support in having this book become a reality.

First, I want to acknowledge my wife, The Rev. Lura Smedstad, for her support, encouragement, and belief in me. She continues to teach me constantly about all the principles I write about in this book. I also want to thank her for her example in having what it takes to get her own book (**Let Spirit Lead Us**, a guide for volunteer directors) into print.

Next, I would like to acknowledge the teachers who supported me in my own transformation and taught me so much about this process. Paul Cutright introduced me to this exciting world when I lived in Hawaii, and he was my first Rebirther. Paul continued to teach and inspire me for years. Layne Cutright and Pamela Ney-Noyes were the teachers in my six-month program of personal transformation. They loved me through lots of times when I was believing that my insane thoughts were real. Dennis DuRoff and Cheryl Raleigh were my teachers during my Rebirther Training. They supported me through my resentment and fears about extending my love to others, and they constantly reminded me of my innocence. Lori Turner, Robin Rider, and Diane Jennings, my teachers in Vancouver, Canada, loved me through my teacher training (and all the guilt that arose in me in the process) and helped me open my heart more fully.

I would also like to acknowledge Dr. Rocco Errico for helping me transform my relationship with the Bible and for solidifying my belief that Jesus' entire message was one of personal transformation. Speaking of the Bible, I would also like to acknowledge the Rev. Frank Giudici, my Bible History teacher at Unity's Ministerial School. He had a high tolerance for angry young rebels like me.

A Course In Miracles is next on my list of acknowledgments. Along with being extremely challenging, it has been an incredible source of comfort. Most of all, it just seemed so familiar. It gave me a framework for my transformation, and it opened me to a relationship with Jesus.

I would also like to thank the Unity Movement (the Unity School of Christianity and the Association of Unity Churches) for teaching me how to be a New Thought Minister and for giving me the opportunity to lead two Unity churches and to found two others. Thank you, also, to the late Rev. Jack Boland, a long-time Unity Minister who was both a friend and a mentor. He introduced me to the concept of transformation through his **Master Mind Principle** prayer program.

Another thank you goes to The Rev. Jerry Stefaniak, a Theophilus Minister and author. His example of writing first one book and then another inspired me to finally begin writing my own book. The person who gave me the last nudge, though, is Mary Russell, a free-lance editor I know who said (as I was trying to convince her to co-write this book), "There is no reason why you can't write the book yourself." Of course, she was right. Thank you, Mary.

Two of the appendices of this book were written as class projects by students in the third-year class of Theophilus Divinity School. The Rev. Lisa Bergerud did the write-up on "How to Feel and Express Angry Feelings." Lisa, the Rev. Janet Rasmussen, and the Rev. JoAnne Sax (now all Theophilus Ministers), working together, wrote "How to Make a Treasure Map." Thanks to all three of you for allowing me to include your good work as part of this book.

Another big acknowledgment goes to everyone who helped me in the editing process. Thank you Lura, the Rev. Joan Gatusso,

Barbara Barker, the Rev. Jerry Stefaniak, Mary Russell, Tracie Loeffler-Donaghy, and the Rev. Stanley Berry. A big thank you also to John Donaghy for all your wonderful work in formatting the book.

I wanted to save my biggest thank you and acknowledgment for last. I especially want to say thank you to my "best non-material friend," Jesus. I constantly turn to you for counsel and help, and you, of course, are always there.

Contents

INTRODUCTION

Prosperity from the Inside Out

This is a book about how to find and express the wealth within yourself so that your outer world will constantly reflect it. It is based on the premise – and many years of experience – that the only way you will have the life you most want, including peace of mind, real happiness, outer prosperity and health, is to discover – to uncover – the real you. And the only way you will fully know the real you is to accept and surrender to your true magnificence.

What This Book is Based On

This book is based on the experience a number of us have had with a set of spiritual principles and how these principles affect our daily lives. The first of these principles is that we are all inherently divine beings, permanently endowed with all the attributes and qualities of our Creator. These inner qualities, such as unconditional love, the power of creation, eternal and unlimited life energy, and the wisdom of the universe, are what make up our inner wealth.

The second spiritual principle is that we each create our own reality according to our most deeply-held beliefs and emotions. Or, to be more precise, God-in-us creates this reality through us according to the direction we provide with our deepest intentions and desires.

What these two principles together mean is literally stunning. They mean that the way to find the only kind of success and prosperity in life which will actually satisfy us is to relax into the deepest part of us, to stop being afraid of what we will find when we look within ourselves. As we open to completely embrace all parts of ourselves, we discover a magnificent being who is very human as well as very divine. We also discover that the world "out there" which we are now creating reflects that inner magnificence.

The Prosperity We All Deserve

Some years ago, I wrote a piece called "What I Deserve." This is a summary of the kind of prosperity we all deserve to experience. It is also our ultimate destiny.

What I Deserve

I deserve to know, to feel, and to express my oneness with God and with all of God's qualities. This means that I deserve to experience myself as innocent, lovable, loving, powerful, fully alive, wise, and bursting with joy and enthusiasm.

I deserve to be at peace with myself and everyone else, and to be living in Heaven now.

I deserve to have all the loving, empowering, nourishing relationships I want to have. I deserve to be a true friend and to have true friendships.

I deserve to experience the abundance of God which is within me, so that I can see this abundance reflected in my life as prosperity and health.

I deserve to know and live my vision. I deserve to fully express my talents and abilities in rewarding and joy-filled ways and to always experience that "to give is to gain." I deserve to be completely open to all God wants me to have.

I deserve to experience myself as valuable and important, and to know that being myself is always enough. I deserve to know my oneness and equality with all people.

This is not a book about how to *attract* or *get* more material things in your life so that you can *feel* better on the inside. This approach is backward and never actually gives any of us the happiness we most want.

This is a book which teaches that the only place in which permanent solutions can be found is within ourselves. If we first decide what we want to *be*, and then we let what we want to be determine what we will *do*, and then we let this determine what we will *have*, we can actually have both the inner life and the outer life we want.

Tapping the Wisdom of Jesus Christ

The basis of this book is the wisdom of Jesus as found in two places. The first place is in the *Gospels*, when they are seen from the point of view that Jesus' entire message was one of personal transformation. The second is his modern-day restatement of his teachings, *A Course In Miracles*.

I'd like to make clear at the start of this book that I do not speak for the *Foundation for Inner Peace*, the publisher of *A Course In Miracles* nor for the *Foundation For A Course In Miracles*, the copyright holders. My views on "The Course" are simply the product of my experience as I have applied their teachings in my daily life.

Several years ago (in 1993), my wife, Lura, and I founded a three-year course of study in Minneapolis called Theophilus Divinity School. The focus of the school's first-year curriculum is deep personal transformation. In this course, we like to include a book on prosperity principles, and I kept looking for one which emphasizes what we want to teach. Finally, I realized that my inner guidance was whispering in my ear that this was a job for me to do.

The Foundation of True Prosperity

The foundation of true prosperity has several aspects, including the following:

1. Money never solves prosperity problems. We all, nearly universally, want to believe that money actually would solve our problems. This simply is not the case. Only inner change can do that. Inner change is what results in our outer lives being improved in any lasting way.

2. There is no way to gather enough "stuff" around us so that we will feel safe. Only a personal relationship with God as our one Source will do that.

3. We can all stop judging our desires. They are all acceptable. That is, they are all acceptable unless they have to do with harming someone or something, or unless they focus on being opposed to something. The universe doesn't work that way. Rather than judging our desires, we can let them keep evolving and do our best to focus on the essence of what we want, rather than on the form. (for example, the "right" marriage partner or job, and not "this particular" one).

Jesus said, "What would it profit someone to gain the whole world and lose his own soul in the process?" If we can get past our old religious programming, we can understand that he wasn't talking about "being bad and then going to some future place called Hell." When Jesus used the word "Hell," he meant "an experience of mental and emotional torment." According to this definition, most of us are all too familiar with Hell. Also, those of us who remember times when we were once living our life as a series of acts (times when we valued the approval of others more than our own self-respect) can understand what Jesus meant when he referred to "losing our own soul."

A Very Poor Rich Man

I once saw an extreme example of someone who seemed to have "gained the whole world and lost his own soul." It was the life story of J. Paul Getty, which I watched on the television program *Biography*. In today's terms, he would have been a multibillionaire, yet he was portrayed as one of the poorest people I ever saw. There was no joy, no satisfaction, no love, no experience of safety, no inner peace – in short, no happiness in having his many millions. As presented in his life story, he was dirt-poor on the inside. In order for prosperity to be "true" prosperity, it must begin with our soul, our essence. It must begin on the inside. As it does, this inner richness will naturally reflect in our outer life, as well.

CHAPTER ONE

Developing a Relationship with Our One Source

F inding the kind of prosperity which includes soul satisfaction as well as outer abundance begins the same way as does everything else in life which is real and lasting. It starts at our relationship with God.

One Source for Everything We Want

How would you like to know that, for everything you want in life, there is actually only one place to look, just one Source? One Source for money. One Source for ideas. One Source for love. One Source for anything and everything you want. Wouldn't that simplify things? Furthermore, how would you like to know that this one Source is the ultimate in kindness and unconditional love? And that this Source wants nothing from you, doesn't test you or judge you or give you crosses to bear or send you to Hell, and asks no sacrifice of any kind from you?

In fact, this one Source is more "on our side" than *we* are most of the time. All It wants for us is our happiness, health, prosperity, fulfillment, and peace. As if all that wasn't good enough, It is also totally available, being within us at all times, constantly there to guide us, create through us, and love us.

We all deserve to know this Source. We each deserve to know the Presence and Power to which we give the name God. But most of us would need to change our concept of God first to even *want* to know Him/Her/It. So in this chapter, I am going to ask you to consider doing just that. If you want to know God as your one immediately available, totally reliable, unlimited Source, it is well worth investing some time and energy in transforming your "God thought."

A God You Wouldn't Want to Know

A wonderful old saying goes, "God created us in His/Her own image, and ever since then we have been returning the favor." In other words, we have been projecting onto God our own traits and characteristics, turning God into a vengeful, wrathful (human) Being who judges and punishes – just like we humans do. The God which most of us learned about in childhood sits on a throne, has a long white beard, sends people to burn in Hell for all eternity, kills people, and causes floods, earthquakes, and lightning. This same God, many of us learned, "gives crosses to those He loves," asks us to sacrifice what we love to do or to have in order to serve Him, and asked His "only son" to die on a cross (as if this was the only way the rest of us could go to a future place called "Heaven.")

How's that for a Source you'd like to get to know? James Michener, in a television interview I saw twenty or more years ago said, "As far as I'm concerned, the most important question I've ever heard asked is: 'Is this a friendly universe?'" As I thought about what he said in this interview, I felt myself agreeing. Whether or not this universe is friendly would tell us whether or not it is safe to relax. Or whether or not there are dark forces trying to trip us up. Or whether or not the universe wants us to succeed.

Thankfully, the universe really is a friendly place. And there are no dark forces "out there" trying to trip us up. Also, there is no being called God "out there" wanting us to leave what we love to do in order to save the souls of people in some far off land. Furthermore, we are all destined to succeed – in the most all-inclusive use of that word. The more we relax, let go, and surrender into our success, the more quickly we find it.

How I Learned to Know God

I'd like to tell you some of my story as a way to share with you how safe and rewarding it is to develop a relationship with your one Source. You deserve nothing less.

My first conscious spiritual experience happened when I was in my mid-twenties. I had been married to my first wife for two or three months, and this was bringing up a lot of fear and rage in me. At the time, I didn't know anything about feelings or about how "love brings up anything unlike itself." I just knew I felt miserable. This was compounded by the job I had. When I got married I had also switched jobs, so that I was now on the road most of the time, staying in cheap motels and trying to sell a line of products with which I was unfamiliar. Also, as a "professional people pleaser," I was terrified of sales so I hated my job.

My first wife and I had begun to attend a nondenominational church just before we got married there. It was in a beautiful setting and had an outdoor amphitheater where services were held in the summer. On one such summer Sunday, the minister was giving a sermon about God's will, saying that surrendering to God often led to a life better than the one we could imagine on our own. At this point, I thought to myself, "Well, why not surrender to God? I can't imagine life being any worse than it is right now." What I actually meant was that I couldn't imagine life *feeling* any worse than it did right then, but the important thing was that I actually had a moment of totally letting go.

When I did let go, I realized that my body suddenly felt relaxed, and that this was a completely new experience for me. Then, I heard a voice inside my head which was as clear as if someone standing next to me was talking. It said, "You are going to be a minister."

If I would have heard that message a year before this, I would not have welcomed it. Instead, it would have fit into my belief that if I surrendered to God, He would send me to a place I didn't want to live. In my childhood, the only people I ever heard say they had asked for God's will to be done in their lives were missionaries who had returned from places like the jungles of Africa and South America. At that point, I had been convinced that if I ever did the same, I would be on my way to somewhere with no indoor plumbing.

By this time, however, I had gotten to know this minister. His life seemed very exciting, so this message was not unwelcome. Actually, it was exhilarating. It also resulted in a great deal of discussion with my wife. When I shared this experience with her, she said, "But Phil, this message could mean anything. It is very possible to be a 'minister' no matter what you are doing for a living." I replied, "Yes, I know it could mean that, but I get the distinct impression that I am going to be an actual church minister."

It turned out that this view was correct, even though it was to be nearly three years before I found a way to start actualizing it. When I discovered the Unity Movement, I found a set of beliefs which fit with me. I also found a ministerial school, at Unity Village, Missouri, which I could attend to learn how to be a professional minister.

Seeing the Bible with New Eyes

Some twenty years later, my second (and current) wife, Lura, and I were to found a ministry named Theophilus Divinity School. The word "Theophilus" means "lover of God, and I am now unabashedly one of those. I am also a lover of Jesus and a lover of the Bible. This wasn't always the case.

The first fifteen or so years of my ministerial career were given to being the leader of Unity churches. When I attended the Unity Ministerial School in the 1970's, one of my teachers said,

"There are two kinds of Unity ministers – those who value having a relationship with Jesus and those who have no interest in that." I was definitely one of the latter. I also wasn't a big fan of the Bible. Once, after a second-year Bible class on some part of the Apostle Paul's travels, I found myself becoming more and more enraged. I stormed into my Bible teacher's office and said, "I hate this book. It has been the source of untold numbers of wars, as well as the excuse for killing and torturing thousands of people. I wish it wasn't even in print."

I raved on for awhile, and then my teacher said, "Your feelings about the Bible are your business, Phil, but what you might want to remember is that nearly everyone on this continent has a relationship with it. Some have feelings about it as strong as the ones you have. Wouldn't you like to at least study it so you can help them with those issues?" Of course, he had a point (along with a great deal of patience!), so I continued to study it. However, I concluded my studies at Unity Village with a very ambivalent attitude toward the Bible. On the one hand, I liked some of its stories and found them very inspirational. On the other, there were many parts I didn't understand and which made it seem like the Bible was teaching things with which I couldn't agree.

During my first year of school at Unity Village, there had been a very bright spot in relation to the Bible. A man named Dr. Rocco Errico had conducted a one-week intensive seminar on "looking at the Bible from a Semitic point of view." Dr. Errico is fluent in several languages, including Aramaic, the language Jesus spoke, and he showed us a new way of looking at the Bible. In this view – which I studied more completely later and which I am convinced is the one Jesus actually taught – there is no place called Hell, no being named Satan or the Devil, and no view of humanity as depraved or in need of saving. God is not a being off in the sky somewhere (although He/She is depicted that way by Old Testament writers whose model for God was an Eastern Potentate). Rather, God is an inner Presence which Jesus calls

"Abba," or "Father." (Actually, "Abba" translates more literally as "Dad" or "Papa.") Jesus' entire message is about "the Kingdom of Heaven," which according to Dr. Errico means "an experience of God's sovereign presence," or (as I would say it) "an experience of oneness with God."

To me, this view of what Jesus taught simply has the ring of truth to it. It says that there is a completely loving, non-punishing God, that there is no place called Hell to fear, and that Heaven is an experience available to us now. I could give you a long look at Dr. Errico's work, but that isn't the purpose of this book. Instead, I recommend that anyone who is interested in healing his or her relationship with the Bible read his books *Setting A Trap For God* and *Let There Be Light*. For now, suffice it to say that Dr.Errico's teaching and that of his teacher Dr.George Lamsa's material has allowed me to have a new relationship with the Bible, and to come to love it. (By the way, the version of the Bible I recommend is the Lamsa translation).

Seeing Jesus with New Eyes

My relation ship with Jesus was altered dramatically by my study of *A Course In Miracles*. Although I initially resisted these books (now one book on thinner paper) as well, I have come to love this course in personal transformation. *A Course In Miracles* says that it is a restatement of Jesus' teachings put into modern language and dictated by Jesus. To me, it is all of that.

At one point, with the thoughts I had about Jesus (that people who wanted a personal relationship with him were engaging in wishful thinking), I was troubled by the statements in "The Course" where Jesus seemed to be speaking in the first person. I had already, however, come to love the material and the change in my life which resulted from studying and applying it. One day, after I had completed a six-month course in personal transformation, and while I was a student in learning how to be a Breath

Integration Coach, I had an experience which was to permanently alter my relationship with Jesus.

A short time before this, while I was reading a book on another subject, something the author said (I don't even remember exactly what) gave me a new insight on how Jesus might possibly be available to everyone at the same time as a guide, counselor, and big brother. One evening, as I contemplated this, I was sitting outside the house where I rented a room. It was evening, and I was enjoying the end of a beautiful day in Hawaii. Eventually, I began to close my eyes, nearly falling asleep.

Suddenly, I had the experience that Jesus was standing about six feet in front of me, and he said, "Why won't you let me in?" Without thinking about it, I responded, "You know, you're right. I've kept you away for far too long." At this point, it was as if my whole body was filled with a current of electricity which felt like two-hundred twenty volts. It wasn't an *un*pleasant experience, by any means. To the contrary, it was intensely pleasurable, so much so that I remember thinking, "I don't know how long I can take this." It went on for several seconds, and then simply came to an end.

The next day, during a Breath Integration Session, he appeared to me again. This time, I simply cried and cried. I felt myself being loved by Jesus and again feeling overwhelmed by the experience. The tears were of gratitude and also of sadness for all the years I wasn't open to this experience.

Since that time, I have had several spontaneous experiences of Jesus coming to me with guidance and love – usually during Breath Integration Sessions. I have also come to rely on him for advice in my daily life. Especially when I am working, I have made it a habit to call on him and to let him be my counselor and guide.

I don't think that these experiences of Jesus make me "special" or different from anyone else, but rather that a relationship with Jesus is available to everyone who wants one. Also, these visits began after I had had an "in my body" experience of oneness with my classmates in my six-month course in transformation, including the realization that I was one with everyone about whom I had judgments. When I have these "visits" from Jesus, it isn't as if he is someone apart from me. It is as if I am communing with the highest part of my own mind, heart, and spirit, as if I am speaking with the self we will all be in the future.

God First – a Prosperity Principle

One of Jesus' "Kingdom of Heaven" teachings contains the first major prosperity principle which I want to share with you. It can be summarized in these words: "Seek first the Kingdom of God and His righteousness, and all these things shall be added to you." (Mt 6:33) In today's English, this sentence would say, "If your first priority is to know God and to align with the qualities of God in you, your outer life will reflect this inner wealth."

So another way to say the first prosperity principle is this: ***The way for us to have everything we want in life is to put our relationship with God-in-us before everything and everyone else in our lives.***

In my life, this relationship with God-in-me, or Spirit (one of Jesus' words for God), comes before my relationship with Lura. It also comes before my relationship with my career, before my relationship with money, and before everyone and everything else in my life. I do not do this because it makes me a better person. I do this because I deserve to know the one Source of everything I want.

The late Jack Boland, a well-known Unity Minister, used to say, "We pray to God as if we were teenagers asking pop for the keys to the car – as if we needed to beg, manipulate, and bargain in order for him to give us what we want." All the while we don't realize that what our soul really longs for – and what Spirit wants for us to have – is conscious contact with God. We want a relationship. We don't realize that there is no need to beg. Once we have this relationship, all the outer stuff we want and need is automatically there, as well.

Jesus, in the Parable of the Prodigal Son, has the Father say to the older brother (the older brother is the "good" one who stayed home and did his duty), "My son, you are ever with me, and *all that I have is yours*." (Luke 15:31) I always like to point out what Jesus did *not* say. He didn't say that all God has *might* be ours *someday*. He said that all God has *is* ours. This means, of course, right now, in this moment.

The God that I know is a Universal Energy, a Life Force, a Presence and Power which treats everyone exactly the same, according to a set of principles which we can all learn. And for each of us, God's presence becomes personal as what some of us call the Holy Spirit, or the Presence of God in each of us. This aspect of God has nothing better to do than to give each of us exactly what we ask for.

What Everyone Wants Most

I would like to emphasize here what I am *not* saying about having a relationship with God. It is not about developing a relationship with God so that we can manipulate the universe (or God, or Spirit, or Divine Mind) into giving us what we want. The approach to prosperity in this book is not about learning to use God. It is about learning how to *co-operate* with God, how to let God flow through us and out into the world. It must begin with our soul. This is the only way we will ever have what we most want – an experience of being "at home." Nearly everyone has had a feeling of "homesickness." Many of us (including me) have actually thought that this homesickness had something to do with finding or returning to some earthly location. Eventually, though, we all discover what it really is about – returning to a place in our hearts where we know God and where we experience being our true selves.

The desire to know our oneness with God is the underlying motivation for all we do in life. No substitute for this will ever satisfy us. This desire drives all our choices (mostly unconsciously) and is our primary motivation in life. It is why we are attracted to certain people, certain kinds of work, and everything else in our lives. So why not make this our conscious intention? Why not consciously decide to put our relationship with God first in our lives?

It is time to go way past the thought of "believing in" or "having faith in" God. It's time to *know* God, as an unconditionally loving, kind, benevolent Force, within us and all around us. I like to constantly remind people, "God doesn't want to take anything away from us – except our suffering. God only wants things *for* us – like happiness, peace, joy, and an experience of abundance."

Five Ways to Build a Relationship with God

Anything we can do to nurture or reinforce our trust in God as our one Source builds the kind of prosperity we want. In this chapter, there are five ways that I want to share with you as to how to practice building a relationship with God as your one Source.

#1 Practice Writing Affirmations

The first "how to" for building a relationship with God is through writing affirmations. I know, I know. Working with affirmations is a technique which is as old as the hills. However, the reason it has been around so long is that it actually does work to produce change in our minds and hearts. This is especially so if it is done the way I learned to do it when I was introduced to Breath Integration Sessions, or, as we called it in those days, Rebirthing. Sondra Ray, one of the pioneers of Rebirthing, wrote a book (no longer in print) called *I Deserve Love*. In that book, there was a chapter on this technique of "writing affirmations." I outline this technique in Chapter Six. It can work to change every part of our lives and experience, including our relationship with God.

When I was trying to create the tuition I needed to do a six-month-long course in personal transformation, I practiced writing affirmations a lot, especially ones about knowing and experiencing God as my unlimited Source. Here are two of the most powerful ones I used to open my heart and mind to knowing God as my one Source.

1. I, Phil, now experience God in me as the unlimited Source of everything I want, especially money.

2. No matter where my money seems to come from, I know it all comes from God in me, Phil.

    (For more prosperity affirmations, please turn to Appendix A. I have included a long list of them.)

The technique of affirmation writing is actually part of a larger one of taking time each day for spiritual nourishment. Some like to meditate. Others like to read. Still others like to write. But what everyone who takes this time each day realizes is that it is a big part of putting God first in life. So give yourself at least a half-hour each day to focus on your relationship with God.

#2 Practice Tithing

The second way to practice knowing God as your one Source is to begin tithing. Tithing is one of the most powerful prosperity-building, relationship-with-God-building activities in which we can engage. It regularly reinforces an experience that God in us is the one Source of everything we want, and it constantly works to heal the sense of separation most of have had between our money and our spirituality.

I first began to tithe when I heard a Sunday lesson on it nearly thirty years ago. I did not begin by giving 10% (the word "tithe" means "tenth"). As I recall, I began with 5%. I still remember how excited (as well as how fearful) I felt when I wrote that first check.

The fearful feeling was from not knowing how my lifestyle could absorb this added "expense" when I was already having trouble making ends meet. The excited feeling was two-fold: First, I knew I was doing something very concrete to demonstrate my faith in God. Second (and somewhat unexpected), was the other feeling of claiming my part in the success of the church I loved.

As I began to plan my giving in this way, I had an experience of the difference between two words which I once heard the Reverend Terry Cole-Whittaker explain. She said that a "donation" is something we can spare, or, in other words, something from which we feel separate. This, she said, is different from a "contribution," which is something included in our monthly financial planning, or, in other words, something which feels like it is a part of us.

When I began to tithe, I also began to feel like I was being a part of the church. When someone's life was changed by learning and practicing its teachings, I felt like I was one of those making this possible. I had not realized how much joy this would bring.

As time went on, I discovered that even though I did not know exactly how it was happening, I did not experience having less money. Sometimes (not always at first) I even experienced having more. It was amazing! It was the first time I had consciously experienced that money, like time, could be elastic.

One day I decided to really "go for it" and commit to giving 10% of the money I earned. Once again, it felt wonderful and scary. Once again, as time went on, I began to have the experience that this practice resulted in having more – not less – of both of inner security and outer prosperity. Even more important, it deepened my relationship with God as my one Source.

Over the next few years, as I studied to become a minister, I learned that the list of people who attributed their success to tithing was a long one. It included such corporate founders as Rockefeller, Kraft, Heinz, Le Tourneau, and H.P. Crowell (the founder of Quaker Oats). I heard the story of a man named Taylor who, in his mid-forties, had experienced many ups and downs and was once again broke. After reading a book on tithing, he decided to try one more venture, this time with God as his Senior Partner. He affirmed this relationship both by tithing regularly and by the name he chose for his store. The chain he founded was, for many years, one of the most well-known department stores in the country. Its name was *Lord and Taylor*.

At first these stories, along with my own experience, drove the intellectual part of my mind crazy. Having begun my college education as a mathematics major, I always wanted to figure out, from a logical point of view, how this could be. It seemed like magic. I later came to realize that this was one of the many ways in which I was trying to understand the spiritual whole by adding up the material parts.

The Two Thought Systems

The more I have advanced on my own spiritual path, the more I know that each of our minds has two major parts. The one is our divine mind or real self, in which we know ourselves as eternally one with God and each other, and in which we know that our true heritage is peace, joy, love, and abundance. The other is our ego identity, or false self. When we're in this state, we feel separate from God and everyone in our lives, we believe in lack, and we believe what our body's eyes tell us, such as that everything has a material cause.

Personal transformation was the inner change I experienced in which I went from identifying with my ego to identifying with and acting from my divine mind. I find that I am always teaching myself, with every action I take, that either one or the other of these thought systems is the truth about me and the world.

The more you, also, teach yourself that you are divine by demonstrating love, oneness, and abundance, the more your outer life will reflect those qualities. The reason that tithers experience having more has nothing to do with magic. There is a spiritual law of cause and effect in operation.

Our most deeply held beliefs and emotions are constantly creating our reality. Our bodies and outer circumstances are, together, like the screen at a movie theater. The projector is the combination of our mind and heart. The only way the image on the screen will change is to change what we are projecting onto it. One reason tithing works so well is that it is a regular and powerful affirmation of abundance. In fact, The Reverend Catherine Ponder has called it "the secret of permanent prosperity." The more it is practiced, the more deeply it changes our inner "projector." The more abundantly we think and feel, the more our lives reflect an abundance of God's love.

Constantly giving 10% of our income is a way to regularly nourish and nurture our relationship with God in us, and to affirm that we actually do have an invisible, yet very tangible and unlimited Source. Money and material wealth are demonstrations of God's love in our lives. In other words, money is simply one form of God's love, just as are ideas, affection, and words of encouragement.

A New Sense of Security

One of the meanings of the word "god" is "cause." In other words, whatever we believe is the cause of our prosperity or well-being is a god to us. If we believe that our job, bank account, spouse, customers, the government, the state of the economy, or anything else outside us is the cause, or source, of our prosperity, we have made these things into gods. We also secretly know that these "causes" or "sources" are unreliable. Banks can fail. Spouses can die or leave. A new product or service can compete with the one we have. Stock markets can take down-turns, and even governments can go broke. But what if we knew that our one constant, unlimited Source is right within us? This knowing gives us a feeling of security unavailable in any other way.

Tithing is a way to build that attitude of trust in God-in-us. It is one thing to say we know that God in us is our unlimited Source and quite another to take an action step which regularly nurtures that knowing. This is so with all spiritual principles.

For Lura and me, tithing means giving the first 10% of our income, before expenses, to the organization, person or group who demonstrate an aspect of God with which we want to affirm our oneness. In other words, we include ourselves as receivers while we are giving. We give to others, and, as we do, we give to ourselves at the same time. We tithe as a way to practice a spiritual discipline. We tithe as a way to nourish our connection to God in us. We also tithe to affirm our oneness with God in others. We tithe "upward," to people or organizations who are successfully applying spiritual principles we want to master. We tithe to people whose lives reflect their oneness with God, those who demonstrate love, abundance, inner peace, harmony, and successfully living their vision. Mostly we tithe to spiritual organizations and teachers. This is because of our conviction that all real and lasting solutions have a spiritual basis.

If you want to begin tithing, start with a percentage of your income which represents a stretch for you, and make it a goal to get to 10%. Make it large enough to be a part of your regular financial planning (a contribution rather than a donation). Take this gift inside yourself and ask God in you where to give it. I recommend giving to people and organizations that are making a difference, those who inspire you by successfully demonstrating spiritual principles. Give where you can say, "I want to claim this as a part of my mind." Give where you can say, "That's for me!" Give to causes and people with which you want to feel joined.

I recommend not tithing to people and organizations because "you feel sorry for them" or because "they need it," unless an experience of neediness is one you want to empower in yourself. If you want to tithe to people or organizations which don't yet look very prosperous or successful, give to them because you believe in them, because you can see their success with your mind's eye. Let your giving empower your belief in abundance, your trust in God, and your idea that money is not separate from your spirituality. Tithe to unconditional love, to success, to prosperity, to oneness. Tithe to relationships, lives, and organizations which work.

When Lura and I tithe, we tithe to those people or organizations who have more fully embodied some aspect of God Mind than we have. We also tithe to constantly remind ourselves that our success is not the product of hard work but the product in our lives of God creating through us. We like to have both of us sign our tithe checks as we decide together who will be the recipient of our tithe. Regular tithing constantly reminds us that God in us is our unlimited Source. It nourishes our trust in God and makes us feel wealthy. The more we feel "rich in God," the wealthier we become in every way, and the more we have to share with the world in which we live.

Tithing Can Seem Miraculous

One story about our adventures in tithing comes from a time when we were living in Vancouver, Canada. We were both in "teacher training" programs, and money seemed tight. We taught and practiced a number of prosperity principles, including tithing. We regularly set aside ten percent of our incomes to give as God-in-us directed. At this point in our lives, Lura's ten-year-old daughter, Meggan, was living with her dad and stepmom. We saw Meggan on weekends, paid child support, and tried to participate in her life in as many ways as we could. This got difficult sometimes, as it does with many blended families, because the other parts of our lives were also very busy.

At one point in this period Lura and I scheduled a camping vacation. Even though we didn't have a lot of money, we felt this was an inexpensive way to give ourselves some needed recreation time. Just before we were to leave, we heard that Meggan needed braces. This was going to cost something like $700, and we were asked to pay half of it.

This seemed to create a dilemma in our lives. We wanted to pay for our half of Meggan's braces. We also wanted to tithe ten percent. We also wanted to go on our vacation. We didn't know how we were going to do all three, but our guidance was to do just that. When we asked Spirit what to do, the answer we heard was to write out the tithe check, to write out the braces check for $350, and to go on our trip. This meant that as we left to go camping on Whidbey Island, just over the U.S. border in Washington, we had less than $100 in U.S. funds. It seemed to me that we were being ridiculous. (This is one of many times I have felt this way when I have listened to my guidance.)

After two days of camping, the money was gone, and I was feeling even more foolish. Then we remembered that friends of ours had a hobby farm just outside Seattle, and that they had invited us to stay in their guest house any time we were in the area. We drove to our friends' home and built a fire in their outdoor fire pit. They came home an hour later and were delighted to see us. In fact, they felt like we were the answer to a prayer. They had just gotten their marriage license and wanted us to do their wedding.

We said we would be delighted to perform this ceremony, and, the next day, we did just that. Our friends told us they felt very grateful to us for supporting them in this large step in their lives and wanted to tithe to us. When we looked at the check, it was the equivalent in Canadian funds of $1,000. Our hearts filled with gratitude as we thought to ourselves, "Had we listened to our egos, we would have believed that we had to choose between giving to others, giving to God, and giving to ourselves. Our egos told us that if we practiced generosity, it would mean we would have less. This is yet another reminder that everything we give is given to ourselves."

#3 Practice Following Your Guidance

A third way to practice knowing God as your one Source is to practice listening to and following your guidance. Many people believe that this is scary, difficult, or both. As to the scary part, remind yourself again that God doesn't want anything from you. God is an Energy which only wants to extend Itself through everyone.

As to the difficult part, it really isn't as hard as those of us who aren't used to it might think. Of course, in the Western Hemisphere, we have spent the last two or three hundred years trying to develop the left side of our brain (the side associated with logic, numbers, and linear thinking), to the exclusion of the other side of us. For many of us, the right side of our brain (the side associated with art, color, wholeness, emotions, and intuition) has gone largely unused. So it will definitely take practice.

One of my favorite phrases from *A Course In Miracles* is the one which says, "Today, I will make no decision by myself." (T. p. 625) This has become a mantra for me. I notice that the more I practice asking the Holy Spirit for guidance and then following it, the easier it becomes to hear this inner Voice.

It's Safe to Trust Your Guidance

One example which comes to mind is an incident which now seems small, but which certainly didn't at the time. Lura and I were in the process of moving from Taos to Minneapolis. We had lined up a fourteen-foot rental truck for a Saturday. We also had arranged for two high-school-aged boys to be at our home at 9:30 a.m. that day to help us load the truck. I arrived at the truck rental agency exactly at 9 a.m., the first customer of the day. It took nearly fifteen minutes for the agent to fill out the paperwork for my rental, and by the time he was finished, there were five people in line behind me.

Just before the agent finished filling in blanks on forms, his co-worker brought my truck around to the front of the building.

As I looked for the first time at the actual size of the truck I had reserved, I thought to myself, "Oh, no! This is going to be way too small. What could I have been thinking? I wonder if it's too late to change to a larger size?" As I was having these thoughts, the service agent was on the telephone, and I had a chance to look at the price list for trucks. I saw that a seventeen-foot truck was only $20 more than the fourteen-footer I had reserved!

My mind raced with a hundred thoughts at once. "For $20 more, I could be sure the truck is large enough. But no doubt I would have to go to the back of the line if I want the agent to redo this transaction. Who knows if they even *have* a seventeen footer available. The boys will be at our house in fifteen minutes. It would take me another hour if I go to the back of the line." Suddenly, I thought to myself, "Phil, take a breath! It's time to go inside and ask the Holy Spirit what to do." So I did. "God," I said, "Is this a big enough truck?" The answer I heard was quiet and certain. "Yes," came the response. So I finished the paperwork and drove the fourteen-foot truck home.

When I got there, the boys were already there, and we started loading. After we had loaded all the boxes, the truck was half full. As I looked at all the other items which still needed to be loaded, I had the thought, "This stuff is never going to fit." But at this point, there was simply nothing else to do, so we kept loading. When we finally finished putting all our belongings in the truck, there wasn't a cubic foot to spare. The truck box was loaded exactly to the rear door, and exactly to the top from front to back. I breathed a silent prayer of thanks and was filled with gratitude.

This is the kind of "small" miracle which happens regularly (although not always so dramatically) in my life as I ask for guidance and then trust what I hear. When I am following the guidance I have heard or felt, I do my best to not believe the fears and doubts my intellect concocts.

#4 Practice Writing Letters To and From God

Yet another way to practice developing a relationship with God is to do something we call "writing letters to and from God." This is a technique I first saw used many years ago at a retreat led by my former teacher, Paul Cutright. In the letters to God, we simply pour out our heart, asking God for whatever answers we have been seeking. In the letters from God, we simply write, "Dear (our name)," and then, on the next line, begin responding as if we could tap into the mind of God for answers. Everyone who does this exercise discovers that, indeed, we can. Lura and I have asked hundreds of people in workshops and classes to do this exercise and to then read their letter from God aloud. As we listen to them, it really is like listening to God speak – every time.

One aspect of this practice is to give your relationship with some situation or person to the Holy Spirit and to then watch what happens. In my experience, the Holy Spirit can literally speak through anyone or anything – the janitor, the president of the company, a billboard, a friend or student calling for support. The important thing is to practice noticing what is going on around you. When you give a relationship or situation to the Holy Spirit, the Holy Spirit always responds.

Of course, the most often-asked question people have is, "How do I know when it is God speaking and not my ego?" There are a few guidelines I've learned to follow, and they all have to do with the nature of God.

How to Know You are Listening to the Voice for God:

- The answer always results in a win for everyone.
- The answer reflects abundance and not lack.
- The answer always speaks for how love is real and how fear is not.
- The Voice for God speaks to us through the desires of our heart.
- The results will look like gain instead of loss.

Ultimately, this question of knowing when it is the Holy Spirit speaking and when it is the voice of your ego always brings to mind the old story of the violinist Paderewski being stopped on the street and asked, "How do I get to get to Carnegie Hall?" The famous answer, of course, is "Practice, practice, practice." This is, finally, how to learn when the Source of your answers is the Holy Spirit. When you look at the results, was it God speaking or was it your ego?

#5 Practice Being Grateful

Last, but most certainly not least, is the practice of being grateful. On the surface, this might not seem like such a big deal. Or, it might seem like yet another "should," a way to be either nice or mannerly. Yet it is none of these. The reason to practice gratitude is not because God needs it – or even likes it. God is, after all an Energy which, says Jesus, "makes the rain to fall on the just and on the unjust." (Mt. 5:45)

No, the reason to practice being grateful is to constantly remind yourself that you are not alone, that you *do* have a Source, one which is constantly giving you what you ask for and leading you toward your happiness. This is a "mind and heart training device" which works extremely well to keep you connected with your Source. So practice saying, "Thank you, God" whenever an answer to a problem or more abundance comes into your life.

One way you can really focus on this tool is to do a "Gratitude List" every day for at least a month. For this month, during your daily "spiritual nourishment time," write a list of everything you can think of to be grateful for today. You will find that this activity feels so good you might well not want to stop at the end of a month.

These are five powerful and concrete ways to claim your connection to God-in-you. There really is an unlimited Source right within you. There is a Presence with which you can commune and co-operate, and which you can come to know intimately. I encourage you to nurture and nourish this relationship every day. You deserve it.

CHAPTER TWO

Uncovering Your Inner Wealth

Many years ago, just after receiving my "call," I found myself without a job. Since the spiritual experience I had recently had seemed so real (even though I didn't yet know what it meant), I didn't know what kind of job to seek. What to do while I figured out what "You are going to be a minister" meant? I wasn't interested, for example, in a "ground floor opportunity." As I went on an interview for one such job, the interviewer asked, "Where do you see yourself in your career in five years?" I decided to answer honestly, ("In a church, leading a congregation") and that, of course, was the end of that. So I had a series of temporary jobs for awhile. One of those jobs came to be a symbol for me that hard work is not the answer to becoming prosperous.

What I Learned from Shoveling Horse Manure

The job was shoveling horse manure in a mushroom growing plant. I made $2.35 per hour for back-breaking work performed in the dark, and then I went home smelling like manure. One evening during this time, as I looked at *Time Magazine*, there was an article on someone who was giving one-week seminars about a then-new theory and technique called "Neuro-Linguistic Programming." The seminars were conducted by a psychologist, and they were mostly attended by other psychologists. The cost of the seminar was $1,000, and there were approximately one-hundred people attending each one.

As I read this article, I thought, "Let's see. This man is making $100,000 per week for having an idea and teaching it, and I'm making not quite $100 per week for doing incredibly hard work in extremely difficult conditions. There is definitely something wrong with this picture. Obviously, working hard is not the way to become prosperous."

At this point, I was also beginning to open to the spiritual side of life. I regularly went to church and attended mid-week classes. At one of these classes, the minister shared a concept which was to become a foundation stone of my belief system. The concept is: *"There is no such thing as luck, chance, or fate. Thoughts are a form of energy, and are always producing results in my world according to a mental/spiritual law."* As I heard this concept, it went "zing" in my body. I knew instantly and instinctively that it was true, even though I had no intellectual understanding of *how* this "law" worked.

Now, nearly thirty years later, this concept is more real for me than ever. Just after I first heard it, however, I struggled mightily with it. Whenever I looked at my own life, and thought, "How could I be creating this in my life," it seemed to work. Whenever my mind went to the six-million Jews killed in concentration camps or even to the 200 people killed in an airplane crash, I would begin to doubt.

The way I would say this concept today is this: *"Our most deeply-held beliefs and emotions are constantly creating our reality."* Sometimes in our work, we draw the following diagram of this idea:

The Screen of Life

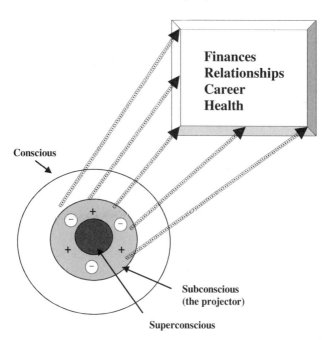

The Superconscious Mind:

The "Superconscious Mind" in the middle of the diagram is our "God self," the deepest, most eternal truth of our being, our innate potential. We are always "created in the image and after the likeness of God" even if we spend this whole lifetime believing we are scum and acting like it.

In other words, the deepest, most fundamental "self" of us is a magnificent being, with all the traits or characteristics of God. This means that no matter how fearful or hateful we have learned to act, we are, at our core, made of love. No matter how weak or helpless we have learned to be, at our core we are beings of incredible power. No matter how removed from our guidance and intuition we have learned to be, we always have access to universal wisdom. And no matter how dead we have learned to act, there is a wellspring of life energy within us waiting to be tapped.

The Projector – the Subconscious Mind:

In this diagram, the projector is our subconscious mind, which is the repository of our most deeply-held beliefs and emotions. It is the storehouse of our assumptions and attitudes. You'll also notice in the diagram that there are plus signs and minus signs. The plus signs stand for beliefs and attitudes which we would most often call positive. Such beliefs as "I can do anything I put my mind to," and "People are innately good," would be examples of positive decisions. The minus signs stand for "negative" decisions. Beliefs such as, "There is something wrong with me," and "People can't be trusted," are examples of negative decisions.

You will notice that around the negative decisions there are circles. These circles stand for emotions such as anger, fear, guilt, and sadness. When we made these self-defeating decisions, usually in childhood, or even as early as at birth or in the womb, these thoughts were surrounded by very powerful emotions. If we decided, for example, that "life is a struggle," it was only after a struggle-filled experience – like that of being born. A birth which was a struggle would have also have been accompanied by a great deal of fear, and probably anger as well.

Even as adults, these powerful emotions are still stored in the body and act like a kind of "glue," holding the old decisions in place. In my own life and in the lives of countless people I've worked with, it wasn't until we began to address our emotional life that any "reprogramming" techniques such as affirmations and visualization exercises began to work with any lasting results.

The reason this part of our mind is called the "subconscious" is that it is below the level of consciousness. Most of our "deeply-held decisions and emotions," the ones which are directly causing the experiences we have in life, are ones we don't even know we have. Why? Because of the pain surrounding them. When we were children, it was painful to bring these decisions to mind. Often, if we cried or yelled when we were hurting, the adults in our lives tried to get us to stop because it activated their pain. So it was easier to just forget that we had thoughts like, "Life is hopeless." Eventually, we forgot that we forgot. But whether or not we are aware of our beliefs and emotional pain, they are still creating our everyday experiences.

The Conscious Mind:

The conscious mind is, of course, the sum of our everyday thoughts. In this part of our mind, we are aware of the beliefs, decisions, impulses, and emotions which we find to be the most acceptable.

The Screen:

The screen itself is our outer life – the state of our health, our relationships, the state of our finances, our career, and all the other parts of our experience.

I like this diagram because it shows how futile it would be to try to change "the way things are" by going up to the screen and attempting to rearrange the images on it. Imagine yourself at a movie you didn't like, trying to change the movie by walking up to the screen and attempting to block out some part of what is being projected onto it. Then, if you are anything like most of us, think of how many times in your life you have tried to do the equivalent thing. Obviously, at the theater and in life, the only way any change is going to be made is if we change the content of the film going through the projector.

So how do we do this? How do we change what is being projected onto the screen of our life? How do we become more prosperous and healthy from the inside out? We do this by under-going a process of inner change called "personal transformation." As Jesus said, "Unless a grain of wheat falls into the ground and dies, it remains alone, but if it dies, it bears much fruit." (John 12:24)

I like the analogy of a grain of wheat falling into the ground and dying to the knowledge of itself as a grain of wheat. This is what personal transformation is like. Other analogies I've used are, "Unless an acorn is willing to die to knowing itself as an acorn, it will never become the oak it always has been in potential." And, "Unless an egg is willing to die to knowing itself as an egg, it will never experience itself as the mighty eagle it could become."

What Does "Personal Transformation" Mean?

One of the dictionary definitions of the word "transform" is "to change the nature, composition, character, or makeup of a thing." This is what is available to us all – to do nothing less than to become something very different than the person we have spent all these years learning how to be. Mystics have for centuries described the ordinary condition of mankind as one of being asleep. They say that most of us are sleepwalking throughout the day, thinking a thousand thoughts that we don't even know we think, feeling emotions we don't know we feel, and deluding ourselves into believing that we consciously "make decisions." Mostly what we do, they say, is to react to stimuli in the same way we always do, with very little in the way of what we'd call a conscious choice.

Mary Baker Eddy, the founder of Christian Science, is said to have remarked that in the book of Genesis, Adam is put to sleep to remove a rib for Eve, and there is no record that he (meaning all of us) ever woke up. *A Course In Miracles* says that we are all asleep and that we are having a very frightening dream. In this dream, we seem to be separate from God and from each other, believing that we are our ego selves rather than our real selves.

The Russian mystic, G. I. Gurdjieff, once said that the way to have the life we want is to be reborn. He went on to say that the only way we could be reborn is to first die to our false self. He continued by saying that the only way we could die to our false self is to first wake up. In personal transformation, this is called "facing our shadow." We could also call it "waking up to our most deeply-held negative decisions and painful emotions."

Another name for this collection of negative decisions and painful emotions is our ego, or our ego identity. In the jargon of personal transformation, the word "ego" doesn't mean what it meant to Sigmund Freud. It is the identity we take on when we perceive ourselves as separate from God and other people. The inner journey called personal transformation, then, could easily be called the one from our ego to our real selves. Our ego identity is based on a lie – that we are separate from God and other people. Jesus called Satan (which is actually another name for our ego) "a liar and the father of lies." (John 8:44) Therefore, everything it says (that we are guilty, that fear is real and love is not, that scarcity is real and abundance is not, etc.) is a mistake. It is the undoing of this mistake that is addressed in personal transformation.

How do we do this? There are lots of "how-to's," but two of the best ways are to accept responsibility for our experiences in life and to do something called "taking back our projections." As to the concept of taking responsibility for our experiences, I discuss this at length in chapters six and seven, so I won't go into it here. Taking back our projections is a way of using our judgments (or critical thoughts) of others as a tool to reclaim and learn to love parts of ourselves we previously disowned.

Judgments: a Tool to Practice Self-Love

I used to believe that my judgments were a form of wisdom, a way of helping me discern what I wanted in life and what I didn't want. However, as I studied *A Course In Miracles*, I learned that all judgments are "projections." Projections are unloving thoughts we have about ourselves which are too painful to face, so we see them in others.

Judgments are a part of our ego identities. When we perceive ourselves as separate from God and people, it is a frightening condition. We can tell we are in our ego mind if we feel defensive. This, in turn, causes us to believe that we need to attack in order to feel safe. Our egos have a variety of "weapons," but perhaps the one egos cherish the most is the one called "judgments."

When we are in our ego mind, we believe that the way to build ourselves up is to tear others down, to find the "flaw" in them. We think that if we can find even one way in which someone is less than us, we will feel better about ourselves. A great many of us spend our entire lives in this state.

There is, however, a tremendous cost to us from living this way. The cost is that we continue to hate ourselves and to hide this self-hatred, even from (especially from) ourselves. We then enter into relationships hoping that others will be able to love us over the top of this self-hatred. We hope they will give us the love we refuse to give ourselves. Thus, it turns out that believing in the reality of our judgments keeps us in a prison of self-hatred.

Literally all judgments (or critical thoughts of others) are projections of unloving thoughts we have about ourselves. As *A Course In Miracles* says (in two places), "Projection makes perception." (T., p. 248 and p. 445) Or, as we often say at our school, "No matter where I look, all I ever see are aspects of myself."

How Judgments Are Formed

How are these judgments formed? As children, we decided that certain thoughts, feelings, desires, and impulses were unacceptable or bad. Our experience told us that if we had these traits, the adults in our life would withhold their love. Therefore, we decided that *having* these traits meant we were unlovable. (When we were children, this felt like a matter of life and death.)

Our child-mind then came up with a solution to this which allowed us to fit in and to function. We simply decided that *we wouldn't have these traits anymore.* We wouldn't do "bad" things because we wouldn't have "bad" thoughts, "bad" feelings, "bad" impulses, or "bad" desires anymore. In other words, we learned to suppress them. We became so good at it that, as adults, we have absolutely no idea they are a part of our mind. (In other words, they are subconscious.) All we know is that we see them in others.

This, then, is what a judgment is – a thought, feeling, impulse, or desire which we see in ourselves and which we have come to believe makes us unlovable. We therefore *disown* it and *project* it onto others. We then live our lives in this ego identity, comparing ourselves to others. We secretly believe we are less than others, so we look for ways to feel better than them, and then we feel guilty about this. We feel separate – from God and from the people all around us.

Healing My Judgmental Mind

When I was a student in my six-month transformational program, I learned that judgments were one of my ego's favorite weapons, a tool I used to keep my low opinion of myself in place. I had a million judgments, or so it seemed to me. As time went on in this course, it seemed to my teachers that I wasn't making much progress in "getting it" about how each judgment I had of another was merely a projection – an unloving thought I had about myself. So one day in class, one of my teachers said to me, "Phil, we want you to go around the room and share every judgment you have with each of the fifteen of us here today. Then, after each judgment, we want you to add, 'What I think that means about you is...' and then after that, 'What I think that means about *me* is...'" She continued by saying, "You can start with me."

As I began this exercise, I felt frightened and very much "busted." I said to the teacher, "A judgment I have about you is that you are fat." "Thank you," she said, and asked, "What do you think that means about me?" I said, "I think it means that you don't practice what you preach in your work." "Thank you," she said. "And what do you think *that* means about me?" I said, "I think it means that you are a hypocrite." "Thank you," she said. "And what do you think that means about *you*?" I replied, "It means that I think I'm a hypocrite, a phony, for being a teacher of inner peace and not feeling like I have any of it myself." "Thank you," she said. "You may continue."

The next judgment I had about her was that she wore rings on her toes. When she asked what I thought that meant about her, I was stumped for a minute. Then I said, "I think you don't care what anyone thinks about how you dress." When she then asked what I thought this meant about me, I replied, "I think the reason I feel judgmental about you having rings on your toes is because of how afraid I am of people's disapproval."

By the time I went around the room, I had accused one of my classmates of being promiscuous (because I was attracted to her and had thoughts of wanting to have sex with her), another of being a "wimp," (because of how powerless I sometimes felt) and the others of a variety of things designed to make me just slightly superior in the eyes of my ego self. As I came to the end of this exercise, my teacher asked me how I felt. "I feel like the scum of the earth," I said. "For the time being, that's probably good," she said. "The only way you are going to heal your self-hatred is to embrace it instead of hiding from it by trying to feel better than everyone."

As I worked on taking back all the "character defects" I had projected onto other people, I had a remarkable experience. A few months prior to this, I had started out this program with the thought, "What am I doing here with this group of losers?" By the end of it, I had an "in my body" experience of oneness with them. I also had a solid experience of self-love. As one of my teachers had said to me, these people were not "special" or different. They were just people. If I could feel at-one with the parts of them I hadn't liked, I could practice accepting myself for having these same thoughts, feelings, and desires. I could also feel at-one with the parts of them I admired. And, if I could feel my oneness with these people, I could also do it with everyone else in my life.

Loving What You've Hated in Yourself

Over the years, I have supported lots of people in taking back their projections so they could learn to love all parts of themselves, including the parts they had hated. In this process, I encouraged them to look at every person in their lives as if that person was their mirror. When one of their mirrors showed them something they liked, I encouraged them to know that this trait was also in them. If it wasn't, they couldn't have seen it in someone else. When one of their mirrors showed them a trait they didn't like, I suggested they ask themselves, "What kind of person would do, say, think, or feel such and so? A lazy person? A coward? A slob? Someone who is mean? Stupid? Selfish? A hypocrite? A wimp? A (fill in the blank?) I would then suggest that they ask themselves two questions.

The first question is, "When do I feel like a (wimp, slob, etc.)? The second question is, "Is it possible that if I wasn't so obsessed with needing people's approval (if, for example, my judgment is that someone is selfish), I would put myself first more often, so it brings up my anger when I see others do it? It is important to look at *both* sides of this question. The projection could be either of two things. It is either a secret thought we have about ourselves, or it is a trait which we would secretly *like* to have more of if we weren't so driven by our fear and guilt.

Nourishing Your Real Self

As I said earlier, the main message of Jesus in the Gospels (and especially in the Parables) is how to live in what he calls "the Kingdom of Heaven," or how to experience oneness with God. In other words, Jesus taught us how to be transformed so we can reclaim our real, most essential selves. And, because of the spiritual principle that our most deeply-held thoughts are creating our reality, it turns out that this is a very important prosperity principle, as well. He said, "Seek first the Kingdom of Heaven (oneness with God in you) and His righteousness (to be in integrity), and *all these things shall be yours as well.*" The word which we translate here as "righteousness" can just as easily be translated as "wholeness, all-inclusiveness, or integrity." Of these, my favorites are wholeness and integrity. In the fullest sense of the word, integrity *means* wholeness. It means to have all of us going in the same direction. The only possible way this can happen is if we uncover and express the divine qualities in us. As we do this, our outer world reflects it.

In two of his Parables, Jesus gives us the following wisdom about how to find and live in this "Kingdom":

"Again, the Kingdom of Heaven is like a treasure which is hidden in the field, which a man discovered and hid. Because of his joy, he went and sold everything he had and bought it. "Again, the Kingdom of Heaven is like a merchant who was seeking goodly pearls. And when he had found a costly pearl (or one pearl of great price), he went and sold everything he had and bought it." (Mt. 13:44-46)

Jesus and the Rich Young Ruler

With these two parables in mind, I want to share with you another Bible story that points to the same teaching. It is the story of Jesus and the "rich, young ruler."

This one I will interpret "metaphysically." If you aren't familiar with the meaning of "metaphysical," don't be alarmed by it. It simply means "above or beyond" (meta) "the literal" (physical). One reason I am sharing this story with you here is that it is often cited as an example of Jesus being "anti-prosperity," which isn't the case at all. If you want to read the story yourself, you'll find it in Luke 18:18-27. I will tell you the story in my words.

A man described as a "rich, young ruler" approached Jesus and asked him, "Good teacher, what must I do to inherit eternal life?" Jesus responded, "You know the commandments. Don't kill, don't commit adultery, don't steal, don't lie, honor your parents, and so on." The young man said, *"All these I have obeyed my whole life."* Then Jesus said, (and I always see him smiling here) "Really! Then there is one more thing you lack. Go, sell everything you have, give it to the poor, and come follow me. You will have riches in Heaven." When the young man heard this he was very sad, *for he had great possessions.*

Jesus said to his disciples, "How hard it is for a rich man to enter the Kingdom of Heaven. It is harder for a rope (not a camel – 'camel' is not a good translation) to go through the eye of a needle than for a rich man to enter the Kingdom of Heaven. *His disciples were amazed, and said to him, "Then who can be saved?"* Jesus responded, "Things which are impossible to men are possible with God."

The key to this story is the question Jesus' disciples asked him when he told them that a rich man couldn't enter the Kingdom of Heaven. If Jesus was saying that people with a lot of money couldn't go somewhere called Heaven after they die, why would the disciples ask, "Then who can be saved?" *They had already released all their material possessions to follow Jesus.* What if Jesus was, instead, talking about another kind of riches?

Starve Your Ego – Feed Your Divinity

To interpret this story metaphysically means to look at all the parts of it in much the same way that some of us interpret dreams – as if they all represent aspects of us. To be sure, if this really was a story about a very wealthy man, then all of us who don't see ourselves as financially rich can dismiss it as being about someone else. But then we would all miss its gifts, because this is a story about how to experience personal transformation.

Metaphysically, a "ruler" refers to our "ruling state of consciousness," or, in other words, our ego identity (the identity we all take on as we perceive ourselves as separate from God and from each other). In this state of mind, we are both blind to our mistakes ("I have kept every commandment my whole life") and full of what we believe to be the absolute truth about "the way life is, the way I am, the way people are." There is something "rich" in us (our ego self), and there is something "poor" in us (our real, essential self).

We all invest the energy of our attention every day in feeding and nourishing either our egos or our real selves. When we identify with our egos, we all have "great possessions." These can be everything from the thought, "My intellect is the source of my wisdom" (cutting ourselves off from our connection with Divine wisdom and creativity) to a belief in victimhood or guilt, to the thought that the way to be safe is to learn how to get good enough at protecting ourselves.

What Are Your "Great Possessions"?

As I said earlier, one of my "great possessions" was my judgmental mind. I thought it gave me a kind of wisdom and kept me feeling just a bit better than everyone else. Another was my view of myself as "special," somehow fundamentally different from everyone else. Yet another was my attachment to being a "noble sacrificer," a person who worked hard now for a reward which would surely come later. All these attachments kept me out of the Kingdom of Heaven in *this* moment. They kept me from having an experience of oneness with God.

As long as we continue to invest our energy in erroneous "deeply held beliefs" (those which are not in keeping with our real selves), we have nothing left to give or feed what is poor or starving in us – our essence. And, until we are ready to be "changed at depth," we go away sorrowing because of our "great possessions."

What Jesus tells us to do in this story is to stop investing the energy of our beliefs in what is (spiritually speaking) false about us – to stop believing that our limiting thoughts are the truth about us. Then we can give all this new energy to what, until now, has been "poor" in us. In other words, it the same advice he shared in the two Parables I mentioned earlier. If we are willing to release our hold on "all that we have" (mentally and emotionally), we will then have energy to invest in, to nourish our true identity. "For the joy of it, he goes and sells all he has and buys that field." When we do this, we, too, begin to have "the pearl of great price," or "riches in Heaven."

How much do you nurture your oneness with God-in-you each day? How much do you nourish your oneness with divine love? Do you let yourself love and be loved as much as you want? How about your power of creation? Do you let yourself in on how powerful you are, or do you continue the spiritual lie of victim-hood? Do you believe that you really can't know your guidance, or do you practice tuning in? Do you practice your oneness with aliveness, with life energy, or do you continue to give space in your life for what deadens your spirit?

These are very practical questions, very concrete and do-able activities for everyday life. In truth, we all have a "rich, young ruler" in us, an ego identity which, if we listened to it would always "go away sorrowing," because *everyone's ego has "great possessions."* Our prosperity, in the deepest and most profound sense of the word, depends on us "selling all we have" and giving the resulting energy to what has been poor, maybe starving in us.

Transformation: the Courage to Face Yourself

This takes a great deal of courage. First, it takes the courage to face our shadow, which many of us have thought would surely result in "death by low self-esteem." This might seem to be hard enough, but this fear is nothing compared to the fear of facing our magnificence, our oneness with God. Oneness with God is both what we all most want and most fear. One of the sayings at our school is, "My fears about expressing myself are fun in disguise." That is certainly true of the fear of claiming and expressing our oneness with God.

What does it mean to "claim and express oneness with God"? For me, there are four main aspects of the Energy we call God: Unconditional Love, the Power of Creation, Infinite Wisdom and/or Intelligence, and Life Energy or Aliveness. There are also many characteristics of God which pertain to us: Innocence, Joy, Beauty, Strength, etc. In this book, I will focus on the four main aspects. I covered Wisdom in Chapter One, and I will cover Power and Life Energy in later chapters. The aspect I want to cover now is the aspect of divine, unconditional love.

Opening to the Wealth of Love in Your Heart

There are two parts of love I especially want to cover here: loving ourselves and loving our creations. Each of these is an essential part of opening to our oneness with God as Love.

First of all, what is this thing called love? Can it be defined? Or can we at least look at what it is in a practical sense? The following are some of my experiences of what love is:

- Love is the binding, cementing, unifying quality of everything in this universe. It is what draws us together.

- Love is what we are created *from* and what we are created *as*. It is not natural to suppress the love in us, and it is not natural to stop ourselves from receiving love. It hurts to hold ourselves back from loving and being loved.

- Love, being another word for God, is not quantitative. There is not "only so much to go around," regardless of what we might have decided as children. (This decision is the origin of competition and jealousy.) The more we express love, the more love there is to express. The more love we receive, the more we and the giver experience oneness with God.

- There are not different kinds of love. All love is God's love being expressed.
- Love is not special. It is not something to be reserved for a special few. Because we are created in the image and after the likeness of God, we each deserve to feel and express love toward everyone, as God does. This is how we experience our oneness with God.
- The essence of love is caring, having respect for, having compassion for, seeing the best in, wanting the best for, and being a true friend.
- Love is a refining fire. It will bring to the surface, in those who give it and those who receive it, any suppressed pain and mistaken decisions so they can be released.
- Love is not sacrifice. It is always possible for us to include ourselves as one of the recipients of what we are giving *while we give it*. This is how we release our attachment to sacrifice so we will feel safer to give and receive all the love we want.
- To love doesn't mean to rescue, to save, or to be someone's Source. It means to empower.
- Love, being an aspect of God, is always unconditional.
- Love is what is left when we let go of fear (as Dr. Gerald Jampolski's wonderful book by the same title suggests). We do not need to look for the love in us. All we ever need to do in order to experience it is to look for the barriers to the awareness of love's presence, and then ask the Holy Spirit to remove them.

The Love in You Can Defeat Any Goliath

There is a wonderful Old Testament (or Jewish Bible) story about the power of love. At least, this story is wonderful if we can look at it metaphysically and look past the blood and gory details of it on a literal level. It is the story of David and Goliath.

In this story, found in 1 Samuel 17, David represents the love in us, because the name "David" means "beloved of God, whom

God loves." If you remember the story, the Israelites and the Philistines are camped across from each other, preparing to do battle. A Philistine giant, Goliath, steps forth and says, "Why don't you send one man out to fight me, and we'll let that fight decide which side wins this battle." Goliath can either represent the fear in us or a problem we are facing. The Israelites, who in the Old Testament stand for the spiritual side of us, are all too afraid to face this seemingly huge fear. In other words, we are immobilized.

David, a shepherd boy, comes to the front lines delivering food to his brothers. He sees what is going on and volunteers to face Goliath. At first he tries on King Saul's armor, at Saul's insistence. (In the Old Testament, kings always represent our ego identities, and egos always think that the way to be safe is to protect ourselves.) David takes the armor off because, he says, "It doesn't fit." (Armor never does fit when we are in a state of love.) Instead, he arms himself with his sling and picks up five smooth stones (one for each of our senses).

As he faces Goliath, the Philistine is insulted. "What am I, a dog, that you send a boy to fight me?" Goliath is described as being six-and-a-half cubits (ten feet) tall. Do you suppose that he, like any problem when we are looking directly at it, only *seems* to be ten feet tall? Also, to our fearful selves, love never looks strong enough to prevail.

David simply slings one stone at Goliath, and it hits him in the center of the forehead (often called our "third eye" or center for imagination). At this point, Goliath has been knocked unconscious. David picks up Goliath's sword and cuts off his head.

Again, if we can get past the goriness of the scene and see it as we would see one of our dreams, (don't you ever have strange visions in your dreams?) as if all the parts of it were in us, it is a beautiful story. What I particularly like about this story is that it so closely mirrors what most of us think about love and attack – namely, that love is weak and attack is strong. On the surface, it can, indeed, look that way. But if we look deeper, at our more spiritual, essential natures, what we find is the reverse. Eventually, love always triumphs over fear and attack.

Learning to Love Yourself

Take, for example, the thought that many of us grew up believing – that it is wrong to love ourselves. Often, we also grew up with the twin thought that the way to improve ourselves and our character was to get good enough at hating the parts of ourselves that we judged.

Perhaps your childhood was similar to mine regarding what I learned about disapproval and love. My dad grew up receiving massive doses of disapproval as a correction device. As a child, he learned that "disapproval is love," and that if you love your children, you show it by never accepting what they do as being good enough. "If you always prod them to be more," this thought continues, "they will become more than they ever would have if you accept them as they are."

Because this was how I experienced being "loved" by my parents, it is also how I learned to "love" myself (and others, for that matter). I grew up believing that it would be a mistake to love and accept myself as I am. I knew there were countless ways that I could (and should) become a "better" person. So, if I loved myself as I was, what motivation would I ever have to "improve"? "The way to become the person I could be," I told myself, "is to get good enough at attacking the parts of myself I want to release."

If you have ever tried this diet of disapproval, you know that, along with the taste it leaves in your mouth, it also doesn't work. There is simply no way to "hate away" the aspects of yourself you don't like. Paradoxically, what works much better is to love these trials, and to love and accept yourself for having them. Love, as it turns out, is far stronger than attack.

Once, while I was working with a counselor, he suggested I "write affirmations" (in the way I outline in Chapter Six) as a part of my personal growth regimen. One affirmation he gave me was, "I Phil no longer need the approval of others because I always have my own." I can still remember the fear that came up in me as I wrote that affirmation. "Give myself unconditional approval? What if I run amok and start hurting people?" (I was not yet in touch with the part of me that would have loved to do just that.) "How will I ever change, stop being jealous of the success of others, stop judging people?" I discovered that this fear wasn't real. Instead, I found that as I learned to love those parts of myself, learned to have compassion for myself, learned to love what I had asked those parts of myself to do – in other words, as I received the gifts from my creations, they gradually dropped away.

Life Treats Us the Way We Treat Ourselves

In my work, I've had a lot of clients who say they want a primary relationship, or want a "better" one than the one they now have. Sometimes these people are quite committed to hating themselves. What they want is for someone to love them over the top of their self-hatred. I remind them that people not only treat us the way we treat them. They also treat us the way we treat ourselves. Often, one of the first affirmations I give to new clients is, "The more I love myself, the more love I receive from others."

In my career, I like to remind myself that I am not paid for how hard I work, nor even for how much I know or how creative I am. I am paid for how much I love myself, how much I actually believe I am worth. So, along with having a wonderful feeling to it, loving ourselves has a very practical side. I find that we are all constantly teaching others (and life) how to treat us by how we treat ourselves.

So one way to become more prosperous is to practice loving yourself. Practice accepting yourself. Write self-esteem affirmations like these:

1. I (your name) always love and accept myself unconditionally.

2. I (name) now experience myself as a lovable, powerful, capable, confident (man/woman).

3. Since I (name) now love myself just the way I am, it is easy for me to receive love from others.

Invest time and money in healing and empowering yourself. Schedule a professional massage. Treat yourself to flowers on your dinner table, even if (especially if) you are the only one who will be eating there this evening. Go on a "self-criticism fast." Have a luxurious bubble bath by candlelight. Stop your car and look at a gorgeous sunset. The list can go on.

Love Brings up Anything Unlike Itself

Don't be surprised if, in the practice of loving yourself, thoughts and feelings of self-hatred come to the surface. Whenever you affirm or accept more of your divine nature, it brings to the surface anything within you which is unlike itself. This happens because the surface is the only place from which we can actually release the mistaken decisions and emotional pain which have been buried in us. I believe it was the Rebirthing Movement, begun by Leonard Orr and Sondra Ray, which coined the phrase, "Love brings up anything unlike itself." In other words, whenever you open your heart to love, whether from someone else or yourself, it activates all of the fear, guilt, and low self-esteem related to whenever you shut your heart down in the first place.

This is true not only for love, but for all the other aspects of our divinity, as well. If we claim or affirm more of our divine power, it temporarily brings up weak and helpless feelings. If we claim our oneness with divine wisdom, it brings up our "stupid" thoughts. If we affirm our oneness with the life energy of God, we might find ourselves feeling tired and dead. If we are winning a lot, it can bring up thoughts and feelings of loss.

This is a temporary condition, one we can simply learn to accept as a part of the process of inner healing. We often call this phenomenon "chemicalization." This term was once used in New

Thought writings to describe the above experience. However, people began to say that they were "chemicalizing" whenever they were ill, so it came to be a confusing term and was dropped from some New Thought texts.

Getting sick is not the same thing as chemicalizing, but getting sick after claiming or affirming more health probably is. Experiencing poverty is not chemicalizing, but going through a period where all your money seems to have disappeared just after doing prosperity affirmations probably is. The most important thing to remember about chemicalization is that it is temporary, simply an indication of healing in progress. It is not a "sign from God" to stop affirming or claiming more of your divinity. You will find that on the other side of this experience, your life will be more of everything you want it to be.

Be More God-Like: Love All Your Creations

Another aspect of learning to love ourselves is learning to love our creations, including (especially) those we now hate. This is actually one of the keys to accepting our oneness with God. Just as, in the Book of Genesis, God beheld everything He/She/It had created, and called it "good" and "very good," so, also, can we learn to love all our creations so we can receive the gifts we want from them.

Since our most deeply-held beliefs and emotions are constantly creating our reality, the converse is also true. If we look at our present reality – our body, our personality, our relationships, and the state of our finances – we can know that they all reflect parts of our subconscious and Superconscious minds.

In each aspect of your life, there may be things you like and things you don't like. Maybe you even hate some of your creations. But there is a way you can learn to love each one of them, and thus accept another aspect of your divinity (unconditional love).

Receiving the Gifts From Each Problem

In Genesis, there is a story about Jacob which often comes to my mind when I am tempted to hate one of my creations. It occurs when Jacob is about to be reunited with his twin brother, Esau, after a long period of estrangement. Jacob is camped by a stream, at a place called Jabbok Ford. The night before his reunion, he has a dream in which he wrestles with an angel. Just before dawn, he says to the angel, "I will not let you go unless you bless me."

In Aramaic, the word we translate as "angel" means "messenger." "Angels from God" are messengers from God. Some of the angels the Apostle Paul mentions in his letters are ministers. These, of course, are also messengers. When I think of this definition, I realize that those creations I call "problems" are also messengers. And, in my life, I find myself having the same experience that Jacob did at Jabbok Ford. I, too, will not let these messengers go until I have received the gift I want from them.

In other words, no matter what situation or condition in life we are looking at, it is here because we want it to be here. We are quite literally so powerful that nothing ever just "happens" to us – we happen it. Why? Certainly not because we are stupid, or because we are masochists. We create what we do because there is some gift we want from it.

Even Illnesses Have Benefits

In the wonderful book *Getting Well Again*, which was published in the 1970's, Dr. O. Carl Simonton and his wife, Stephanie, spoke of the work they did with cancer patients. Carl was an oncologist, and Stephanie was a behavioral psychologist. They began to work together and presented some radical ideas, one of which was that the cancers their patients were dealing with were actually there because the patients unconsciously believed that they "needed" them for some reason. For example, a classic case often cited in this kind of work is one in which someone feels he is in a "double bind." He has some decision to make, and neither option looks good. Having an illness, then, can be a way to not have to make a decision.

The Simontons suggested that each patient write down the five or ten "biggest benefits" they had received from having the cancer. As the couple heard the responses, it seemed clear to them that their theory was true. They had a remarkable recovery rate with the patients who fully participated in the regimen of combining both traditional cancer treatment modes, and this type of psychotherapy.

Then they began to do this exercise themselves. They wondered what would happen if they looked at any illness they had had and wrote what had been the "five biggest benefits they had received." Again, they felt that they were onto something. It seemed to them that their bodies had responded to their unconscious intention and had given them what they believed they needed.

There Are Angels Everywhere

As I studied this concept, I asked myself, "Is it possible that this same idea would apply in *every* area of life? As I began to look at the different situations and "problems" I had, I discovered that the answer was an unqualified "yes." No matter where I looked – my health, my weight, my acne, the state of my finances, my relationships with people, the kind of neighbors I had – I could, if I looked deeply enough, find that each area I disliked was an "angel." It was a situation that had come to me with a gift in its hands. No matter how intensely I tried to "hate these things away," I had the same experience as Jacob. "I will not let you go until you bless me." This is, of course, the same idea as the phrase which Werner Erhard is said to have coined: "Whatever we resist persists."

If you believe that the state of your finances or your career or any other part of your life is not what you want it to be, I invite you to do the same thing I have done when faced with something

I call a "problem" – write down the five biggest benefits you receive from having it in your life. Once you see what it is you asked each situation, or "creation" as I call them, to give you, it will be easier to love it. And anything you love will either expand (if it is an aspect of your divinity) or dissolve once you have received the gift you wanted from having it in your life.

Letting yourself feel and express the love in you is just one part of getting in touch with your inner wealth and abundance, the richness of God within you. Due to the operation of spiritual law (we are always creating our reality through our most deeply-held beliefs and emotions), the more you experience this inner wealth, the more your outer world will reflect it.

CHAPTER THREE

From the Inside Out

One of the most powerful prosperity principles we can practice is to align our minds with God's thought system of abundance. According to *A Course In Miracles*, there are really only two thought systems for us to choose from. There is the ego's thought system of scarcity, and there is God's thought system of abundance.

The real purpose of our life on Earth is to support us in moving from the one to the other. When I think of this journey, there are two pictures that come to mind from the Bible. Looking at the Bible metaphysically, its history becomes "his story" and "her story" – the story of our evolution.

The first picture is from the first part of Genesis. Adam and Eve get removed from the Garden of Eden after they eat from the "Tree of the Knowledge of Good and Evil" (after they begin to judge). Then Adam (who represents the mental side of each of us) hears God tell him that from now on he will work very hard ("by the sweat of his brow"). Eve hears from God that "in pain and suffering will you give birth." Eve represents the emotional side of us. When we experience ourselves as separate from God, the thinking side of us works very hard, and our emotions suffer as we try to give birth to anything new. This is how life is for us until we awaken to our oneness with God.

The second picture is one of Jesus feeding 5,000 people when all that was apparent was enough food for one person's lunch.

Along with all he was and is, Jesus also represents something in each of us. He represents "a conscious experience (not just awareness) of oneness with God." For most of us, this is a state of potential. Jesus, in becoming the Christ (the example of what we all can be), expressed all the qualities of God (like Love, Power, Wisdom, Aliveness) on a daily basis. Because of all he did, he represents the future of us all, our destiny. In this future state, our minds and hearts are filled with God's thought system of abundance.

In the last chapter, I said that Jesus had taught us much about personal transformation, or the process of inner change which results in us living in the Kingdom of Heaven (experience of oneness with God). One large how-to is "selling all our ego investments and giving the resulting energy to what has been poor and undernourished in us – our real selves." Nowhere is that more important than it is regarding the concepts of scarcity and abundance.

How to Tell When You Are in Your Ego Mind

How do we know when we are identified with our ego and when we are identified with our real self? Here are some of the ego's properties:

First of all, the ego is not a "something" in and of itself. It is a state of identity. It is who we think we are when we experience ourselves as separate from God and other people. It is who we believe we are when we feel separate from the love, the aliveness, the power, and the wisdom in us. It is who we think we are when we see ourselves as "only human" (as important as it is to embrace our humanity).

When we identify ourselves as our ego, we think we are a body which contains a mind, rather than the other way around. We look with our body's eyes and believe what they report as the truth. The first thing our body's eyes report is, of course, that we stop at our skin and others start at theirs. So in the view of our body's eyes, we are obviously separate from one another. As a body, we can be hurt, and we can hurt others. This means that both fear and guilt are real. Because of the way our minds work, we can either believe that love is real and fear is not, or we can believe the reverse, but not both at the same time. When we are in our ego mind, we always doubt that love is real. And, because that is the experience we are looking for, that is the one we find.

When we are in our ego mind, there is another way we practice the "scarcity principle." We think there is something missing in us. We are, we think, somehow incomplete. Because we are incomplete, we must look outside ourselves for what we need to complete us. Maybe it's a relationship or the right job. Maybe it is surrounding ourselves with enough "stuff" to make us feel safe and happy. As much as I love material prosperity, the problem is that no matter how much stuff we surround ourselves with, it will never fill up the empty place we have in our solar plexus when we think there is something missing in us.

When we are in our ego state of mind, thinking we are a body, it means that when we look around, everything seems to be made of physical material. This means that there are only so many pieces of the pie. So, the more others have, the less we have. The more others win, the less possible it is for us to win. Therefore, we think, the way to have what we want is to be defensive and competitive. We believe we must protect what we have so others don't take it away from us. If we turn our back, we think, someone will take it away from us. The way to have what we want is to have an edge, to manipulate, to be smart enough and clever enough. It's a dog-eat-dog world. We can lie, cheat, and steal. So long as we don't get caught, our ego tells us, there is no problem.

Egos literally live by comparison. When we are in our ego mind, we are always looking for how we are "better than" or "less than." We never see ourselves as "equal to." We are always looking for some way we can be "one up" on you, some way we can build ourselves up by tearing others down.

From Perceiving Lack to Seeing Abundance

A Course In Miracles teaches that living this way is a kind of insanity, that we are not in our right minds when we have to live such a fear-based life. Not that it isn't "normal." Most of us can identify with at least some of the above thoughts, and, if we look around, it isn't hard to see this state of mind on all sides. My wife, Lura, likes to say, "This kind of experience might be normal, but that doesn't mean it's natural."

When I think of choosing between which reality – God's or my ego's – I want to know as real, it brings to mind an experience I had while I was living in Florida in the late 1970's. It was during one of the "energy shortages" which resulted in all of us waiting in long lines at gas pumps. When we finally got to the pump, we could only buy a few gallons at a time, and the prices were far higher than those we were used to.

At one point during this period, Hurricane David swept ashore and, for a few days, churned up the east coast of Florida. Somewhere in the news coverage of this storm, I remember reading that every day Hurricane David was generating enough power to supply six months worth of the electricity used in the United States.

Clearly, there was no shortage of energy. There may have been a shortage of *available* energy, but there was, and always will be, an abundance of energy. What there really was a shortage of was ideas of how to tap into and use the energy which was always there.

I once heard a speaker quote the great thinker and inventor R. Buckminster Fuller as saying "There are enough *known* resources on planet earth for all of us to live on a level equivalent to being billionaires, provided (and this is, of course, a very large "provided") that we would learn how to share them with each other."

The fact that some of us can't see this abundance doesn't mean it isn't there. When we are in our right mind, our thoughts are aligned with the thought system of God, which is entirely based on abundance.

How to Tell When You Are in Your Right Mind

When we are spiritually sane, we know that we are not a body which contains a mind or soul. We realize that we are Spirit, an idea in the Mind of God. *A Course In Miracles* says that, as ideas in the Mind of God, we are still one with God because ideas do not leave their source.

In this book, I am sharing ideas with you. To the best of my ability, I am giving you my ideas on a certain subject. As I share these ideas with you, I don't lose them. I still have them, even if you do also. Not only that. As I share them with you, they actually become more real to me, as well. So, when I am spiritually sane, I realize that the way to experience having is to give, since anything and everything I give is, like me, essentially an idea. As I extend the love in me, it expands, and I find myself living in Heaven. (One meaning of the Greek word which we translate as "Heaven" is "to expand.")

When we are aligned with God's thought system, we realize that love is real and fear is not. Fear is not a thing, but a "no thing." It is the apparent lack of love. No matter if our body were harmed, or even destroyed, we are literally invulnerable, and so is everyone else.

When we are in our right mind, we realize that nothing "happens" to us that we don't want to have happen. We know that we create our own reality (or that the power of God creates it through us). This means nothing less than that we don't have to defend ourselves from those around us. Instead of defensiveness, we can practice having an open heart, which is a key to having the love – in all forms – that we want. We can practice knowing that people are either expressing love or they are issuing a call for love, and we can respond accordingly.

When we are spiritually sane, we realize that we have but one Source – God in us. This Source is, we know, unlimited, and supplies our every need and desire in an abundant way as we extend the love in us, as we contribute to the world in all the ways we love to give. We understand that the way to have the prosperity we want is to practice creation, instead of believing it comes to us by "the sweat of our brow" and with a great deal of pain.

When we are in our right mind, we practice the principle of win/win in all our dealings in life. We realize that everything we give is given to ourselves, and that everything we do is done to ourselves. We are one with everyone in our lives, each of us on the planet a cell in the body of Christ (to use Paul's term). To align our mind with God's is to realize that God only has one child – all of us together. This means that God can't possibly support one person winning at the expense of another.

When we are spiritually sane, we realize that we never actually have to make a decision. What we do instead is listen to our guidance. The Holy Spirit in us is constantly guiding us toward happiness and abundance. The path of ease is to let ourselves have this guidance, instead of endless hours of "trying to figure things out."

Being Nourished from Within

This is where Jesus lived – in the realm of God's thought system. Once, when the disciples asked him, "Master, aren't you hungry," he responded, "Actually, I have food to eat that you don't know about." (John 4:32) He experienced being nourished from another dimension, from the realm of Spirit. When he was in the desert being tempted by Satan (his ego, in other words), he heard his ego mind say, "If you are so hungry, turn these stones into bread." Jesus responded, "Man doesn't live by bread alone, but by every word which proceeds from the mouth of God." (Mt. 4:4) There is a kind of nourishment we experience when we live our lives based on God's thought system.

Jesus also said, "No one can serve two masters. You'll either hate the one and love the other, or you'll regard the one and despise the other. You can't serve God and mammon." (Mt. 6:24) Many people think that the word "mammon" must mean money. A more useful meaning is "the realm of material cause." If we believe that anything outside us is the cause of our happiness, we are making it into our source. If we do that, we can't put God first, and then nothing in life works as well.

To use a personal example, if I put my relationship with Lura before my relationship with God in me, or if I put my career ahead of my relationship with God in me, I am trying to serve two masters. I begin to compromise my values and make decisions based on fear. I love my wife a lot. I also love my career a lot, but I practice knowing that my *Source* is within me. (At least, this is what I do when I'm sane. If I get into my ego mind, I ask for support. Then I again practice putting God first as soon as I "come to myself.")

Jesus also said, "In the world you have tribulation, but be of good cheer. I have overcome the world." (Jn. 16:33) He encouraged us to be "of" somewhere other than "the world" because this is how we maintain our sanity. Where, then, is this "somewhere else"?

A *Lesson from a Two-Dimensional World*

To begin to describe where we can practice being from, I will tell a story which comes from Victorian times. I saw it published in the book, *The Aquarian Conspiracy*, some twenty years ago, and ever since then it has seemed a wonderful way to introduce this other dimension of life.

The story is about a place called "Flatland," which is a two-dimensional world. This means that while there are both length and width, there is neither height nor depth, no up and no down. From a three-dimensional perspective, looking down on this world, it looks like one large architectural drawing, with lines defining the borders of streets and houses. The residents of Flatland look like dots, and, as they move, they look like skate bugs moving across the surface of a pond.

One evening, as a family in Flatland was having dinner, they had a visitor from Spaceland. The visitor was a giant from the realm of three dimensions. He reached down, picked up the father of the family, and gently brought him close to his face so he could get a good look at the creature. Terrified, the Flatlander cried, "What is happening to me? Am I crazy? Is this hell?" "Neither one," The Spacelander replied. "This is knowledge."

With this, he gently held him as he guided him on a tour over his own house and village. He said to the Flatlander, "See how your world looks from here? There is so much more to life than what you have seen – a whole other dimension, in fact." He then pointed to objects in the three-dimensional world and said, "See? Rocks, trees, clouds, rivers, grass. There are so many things here to see."

After this tour, and after reassuring the Flatlander again that he was not crazy, he set him back down at his dinner table. His family had been frantic. To their perception (since there is no "up" in this land), he had simply disappeared. Then, just as suddenly, he had reappeared. They asked him where he had been. He didn't know how to respond. There were no words in his language for "up" or "down," so he said, "I was, um, sideways to sideways." He then tried to tell them about the incredible adventure he had just had, and about how much more there is to the world than what they know.

His family and most of the others to whom he told this story thought he was crazy. They tried to get him to see that he was just hallucinating or that he must have been having a dream. Even though his family saw him "disappear," they convinced themselves that this must have been some kind of optical illusion. Eventually, he was labeled as a lunatic and put into an institution for the insane, because he wouldn't stop telling people that there is a whole other dimension to life than the two of which they are aware.

The Fourth Dimension: Accepting Your Waveness

When I think of this story, I think of Jesus, having discovered a fourth dimension he called "The Kingdom of Heaven." Since language is based on common experience, and since he was the only one who had actually experienced this dimension, he then tried to tell people about this dimension. I can imagine him thinking, "How shall I describe this experience? Let's see, 'The Kingdom of Heaven is like ...leaven in a loaf of bread... a woman who won't stop bugging a judge... a dragnet... a pearl in a field.'" No matter how he described it, he probably got a lot of blank stares. Even now, two thousand years later, most people don't realize that he was talking about something available here and now, a realm of wholeness, abundance, and oneness.

Another way to talk about a fourth dimension is to describe some recent research in the field of quantum physics. In this research, it is somewhat difficult to describe the smallest sub-atomic particles we can observe because they do not always act like particles. Sometimes they act like waves.

Most of us are more familiar with particles than we are with waves. Particles take up space. They have weight and mass. We can point to items made of particles and say where they begin and end.

Waves are forms of energy with which we may not be so familiar. What we are most aware of with waves is their effect, as in radio waves. For example, if we were to turn on a radio where we are right now, it would produce sound. If we tuned it to a different channel, it would play a different group of sounds. We say that this is because the room or area where we are is full of radio waves of different frequencies. We can't see them, and they are "omnipresent" (at least within range of where their signal originates), whether or not we are tuning into them.

These radio waves have another property. If we were to gather up twenty radios and tune them all to one station, they would all play as loudly as if each was the only set in the room. We see this phenomenon each time we walk past a hundred television sets in a department store airing the same show. This means that in the realm of waves, there aren't just "so many pieces of the pie." *It means that when one of us has more, others don't have to have less.*

There is yet another property to these waves. They are affected by thought. As it turns out, there is simply no such thing as an "objective observer" in scientific experiments. Research has now shown us that the wish or desire of the experimenter helps to determine the outcome. Things tend to go the way the experimenter wants them to go, or in accord with what he or she believes.

What does all this tell us about the nature of things? Remember, we and everything we can see with our body's eyes are all made up of these tiny "wave-particles." This means that there is a dimension of "reality" in which quantity means nothing. In this dimension, there is no such thing as lack. It also means that in this dimension, everything is affected by thought, belief, and intention.

Opening to Our Inner Senses

There was a time in my life, some twenty years ago, when I was not able to see auras, or energy fields, around people. For several years, I had been aware that they existed, as shown by Kirlian photography. I just was not "able" to see these energy fields. Then one day, while a meeting took place in my office, I was pondering this. The light was somewhat dim, and I decided to practice looking just past one of the people there to see if I could see his aura. Sure enough, I could make out a very definite shape of energy around the person. Then I decided to see what would happen if I told myself I didn't want to see it. It seemed to go away. This type of seeing depended on my willingness to see it, and on my belief that it even existed. I had to give my permission in order to be able to see. For a time after this first experience of seeing auras, I was fascinated by this new "ability" (which, of course, had been there all along) and practiced seeing them around everyone. These days, since I am much less fascinated, I only see them when I make a conscious effort. I simply know that they are there.

This same kind of willingness is important with respect to other areas of spirituality and/or psychic abilities, as well. It is quite easy for me now to tune into how someone is feeling emotionally, but this was not always the case. Before I got in touch with how much emotion I was suppressing, and before I learned how to express my feelings appropriately, I was completely unaware of how I or anyone else was feeling. Now, when I tune in, this information is right there.

The same is true for being able to hear people's thoughts. We regularly include, in our second-year classes, lessons in how they can send mental messages to their classmates (when, for example, they are on a logistics team together and need to get a teammate's attention silently while a workshop is in progress) or to a client during the deep-breathing part of a Breath Integration Session. When people first experience that this is a real phenomenon they are usually amazed. "Wow! I can actually send and receive messages without talking!" Then, it gradually becomes an everyday part of their life. Once again, this experience is subjective. It only happens if we are willing, if we give our consent and want to believe it is possible. This is also, of course, how it is with listening to our guidance. We first must believe it is possible and want to hear what the Holy Spirit has to say in order to hear it.

In my life, the experiences of clairaudience (inner hearing), clairvoyance (seeing with inner sight), and clairsentience (feeling what others are feeling) are no longer part of the realm of oddity or "special" gifts. They are simply an indication that we really are all part of one mind. They are also indications that there is another dimension to life, one to which we can open if we give our permission. If we say, "Yes, I am willing to see the abundance behind the appearance of lack," or " I want to see the oneness beyond the appearance of separation," or "I insist on seeing the wholeness beyond the appearance of brokenness," we can experience this new dimension.

Properties of the Fourth Dimension

In the fourth dimension, nothing is diminished by giving, because in the fourth dimension, everything exists as an idea. As I said earlier, the more an idea is extended, the more real it becomes. In the fourth dimension, we manifest not through hard work and enough suffering, but through creation. In the fourth dimension, we have the experience that there are infinite amounts of everything, because everything is comprised of energy, and there is simply no lack of energy. In the fourth dimension, there is no such thing as competition. No one feels the need to manipulate, use others, or to play win/lose games. There is no envy or jealousy because there is plenty and everyone knows it.

In the fourth dimension, there is no need for secrets because we know we are all parts of one mind. Neither loss nor fear are real because we realize that we are spirit manifesting through bodies for a time, rather than bodies which contain a soul or mind. In the fourth dimension, we don't use defenses because we realize that if we are defending ourselves, we are also attacking ourselves. Besides, we consciously know that nothing happens to us except that for which we ask. Since we realize our oneness with each other and with God, we know that we only have one will – God's.

In the fourth dimension, we know that love is an idea, which means it only increases as it is shared, so we don't reserve it for a "special" few. We don't think that we will run out if we give too much or receive too much, so we let ourselves express and receive as much of it as we want.

What is this fourth dimension? It is nothing other than the Kingdom of Heaven which Jesus came to teach. It is the experience of oneness with God and oneness with everyone on earth. I hope it is becoming increasingly clear how this relates to practical matters like how to pay the rent.

A Man Who Was Stuck in the Third Dimension

One day, when I was the minister of a church in Florida, a man came to see me for counseling. He had a hair styling shop and was having a difficult time making it in business. His view of the problem was that there was simply too much competition in town. He had reduced his prices several times, and still couldn't attract enough people to his shop. Besides, even with his low prices, people still complained about how much it cost to get a haircut.

I asked him how it would be if he simply stopped trying to compete. I asked him to visualize himself charging rates at the top end of the scale for haircuts, and I told him that if he was going to do this, he would have to be passionate about his work and do it with excellence. He proceeded to tell me why everything I had said would be impossible for him. My experience of him was that, like the rich, young ruler who came to see Jesus, he went away sorrowing because he, too, had "great possessions" – an attachment to suffering and complaining, a belief in lack (especially in himself), and low self-esteem.

Had this man been willing to live in the world of creation instead of the world of competition, the world of ideas instead of the world of "the sweat of my brow," he could have had a much easier time of it in life. The same is true for us all. We can, to paraphrase Jesus, learn to be *in* the world of particles without being *of* the world of particles. We can access our "waveness" and live from our oneness with it while we express ourselves fully in the world of particles.

It is, of course, as important to learn to function as a "particle" as it is to learn to access our "waveness." Each of us is here on the planet by agreement. We have all agreed to live according to the laws of gravity, inertia, etc. We also have agreed (consciously or unconsciously) to pay taxes and to be citizens of the country in which we live. We need to take care of and love our bodies, places of living, and means of transportation. Also, in each of our chosen ways to express ourselves, there are limits to the freedom we have. If we are going to experience success in any chosen field, we have to be willing to accept those limits. It is as important to master being "in the world" as it is to master *not* being "of the world."

Nourishment for the Soul – Feeding the 5,000

There is a Bible story which is a wonderful example of living from the fourth dimension. It is the story I mentioned in an earlier chapter of Jesus feeding 5,000 people. This is the only "miracle" which is mentioned in all four gospels, so it is an important story. Here is a metaphysical meaning of this story.

Symbolically, Jesus represents the Christ in each of us, a "conscious experience of oneness with God." The disciples in this story can represent the human side of us, our ego minds. It begins with Jesus teaching in a wilderness area, far from the nearest town. It is late in the day, getting on toward dark, and Jesus says to the disciples, "We need to give these people something to eat." Although each gospel's version of the story is different, in one account the disciples' response is, "The place is desert and the time is past." Or, in so many words, "There isn't enough, and it's too late to do anything about it. Where in the world would we get enough food to feed all these people? We'll have to send them away." Can you hear yourself in this disciple's reaction, especially when you are completely identified with your "particleness"? I certainly can.

Jesus says, "No, don't send them away. Have them sit down. What do we have here to share with them?" The disciples say (again, in so many words), "We have only five loaves of bread and two small fish." They are caught up in looking at the appearances of the situation, looking at what is apparent in the three-dimensional world. Jesus asks them to give the food to him and he "looks up to heaven."

In another story, Jesus says, "You say there are four months and then comes the harvest. I say unto you, 'lift up your eyes, for the fields are even now ripe unto the harvest.'" (Jn. 4:35) If we were to continue on with this thought, we might hear him conclude that sentence with, "if you could only see it." So, in this story, Jesus "lifts up his eyes" to heaven, or to the fourth dimension. He takes his eyes off the appearance of lack, and points his vision toward the realm where all the supply comes from. He gives thanks for abundance, he blesses what he has, and he begins to share it with everyone there.

Seeing the Story Through Mid-Eastern Eyes

Dr. George Lamsa, the Aramaic Bible scholar, points out that in this part of the world, exaggeration is a normal part of conversation, and people do not think of it as lying. Its intention is to emphasize, not deceive. Dr. Lamsa's student, Dr. Rocco Errico, recalled a time when Dr. Lamsa (who was from Iran, and spoke Aramaic as his native language) had spoken at a hall which held about 700 people. In a phone call to Dr. Errico, Dr. Lamsa excitedly told him how successful his lecture had been. "There were two or three thousand people there," he said. Dr. Errico knew how many seats there were in the auditorium. He also knew that this was not an attempt on Dr. Lamsa's part to deceive him. It was simply said to emphasize how successful he felt the lecture had been.

When this story is told as the "feeding of the 5,000," it doesn't mean that there are literally 5,000 people there. (As the story is written, there were many more there anyway. In at least one account, it says, "There were 5,000 men there, besides women and children.") It means that, as the writers saw it, there were a *lot* of people.

Dr. Errico also pointed out, at a seminar I attended, that these people were not so naive as to be out in the middle of nowhere with no food. He said that at this period in history, the people would have been dressed in layers of clothing. If they were traveling, they would have been hiding food somewhere on their person so they wouldn't lose it to robbers. The real miracle of this story might well have been in getting all the people to share – so much so that there were twelve baskets of food left over.

Perhaps you have heard this story referred to as the one where Jesus "multiplies the loaves and fishes." However, if you look at all four versions of the story, there is not one mention anywhere of "multiplying" anything. Does it really matter how the people got fed? Is one kind of "miracle" really any less impressive than another? It could easily be that *how* the people got fed is beside the point. The disciples, representing for each of us the "human" way of looking at the problem, couldn't see the abundance which was there. Jesus, as he "looked up to Heaven" gave thanks because he could. He saw the reality of the fourth dimension. Then he began to break bread and pass it out. In other words, he began to demonstrate generosity and to share all he had. He began to "act as if." He began to demonstrate abundance. Then, because of the power of his presence and his actions, everyone else began to share what they had, and everyone got fed.

There is Always a Next Step

One of the powerful lessons in this story is that, no matter what problem or lack any of us are facing, there is always a starter. There is always something we can do, a next step to take. Then, after we take that one, we will hear our guidance say what to do after that. And so on. As we do this, the people get fed, the problem gets solved.

In the Bible, bread represents nourishment of whatever kind we need. Jesus, when he was being tempted by his ego, said, "Man does not live by (physical) bread alone, but by every word which proceeds out of the mouth of God." (Mt. 4:4) In other words, our essence is nourished by listening to our guidance. There is an increase in energy available to us if we are in touch with the fourth dimension. The number "five" means that there is food, nourishment, or nutrition for our five senses. (The zeroes are just for emphasis). Our five senses are either being "fed" by looking inward for Spirit's take on what is true in the world – looking to the realm of the fourth dimension for what's real – or they are being slowly starved by looking at the three-dimensional world for causes, and for what's real and true. The fact that there are three zeroes after the five means that we have become very hungry. In fact our soul is starved for nourishment, but the Christ within (conscious experience of oneness with God) is very capable of feeding that hunger.

Fish, in the Bible, are often a symbol for ideas. Fish in the sea can stand for ideas in the mind of God. There is another wonderful story where the disciples are out "fishing all night." (Jn. 21:3-6) "All night" means "in the dark." It means being unable to see or perceive the solution. This state can, of course, last for a moment or for years. In the story, Jesus (conscious experience of oneness with God) shows up in the morning on the shore. (The light dawns when we remember who we are.) He says to them, "Pick up your nets and then let them down on the right side of the boat."

What possible difference could this make? Moving nets three feet one way or another is usually not a prescription for catching fish. Have you ever heard your guidance say something that doesn't seem to make any sense to your logical mind? I certainly have. When I follow it, wonderful things happen, just as they did to the disciples. When they, no doubt having been through this before, surrendered immediately to Jesus' suggestion, there were so many fish (ideas) there was hardly a place to put them.

In the story of feeding the 5,000, there are two fish. The number two represents the great concept of duality – plus and minus, positive and negative, male and female. In this story, it also represents "yes and no" – what to say "yes" to in life, and what to say "no" to in life. This is our constant choice. As it relates to ideas, it means which of them to say "yes" to (the realm of Divine Mind, or the thought system of God), and which of them to say "no" to (the realm of the ego, or the thought system of lack, separation, and fear).

Practice Living in the Fourth Dimension

There is an easy way to tell if you are saying "yes" or "no" to the fourth dimension. When you find yourself looking at people, do you practice seeing their bodies or do you practice seeing the person? It is only possible to see one or the other. If you are looking at bodies, it means that you are seeing with the eyes of your ego mind. Egos always see differences and can only think in terms of "better than" and "less than." Egos always attempt to answer the questions, "Is there some way I can use this person?" and "Is there something I can get from him or her?"

There was a time in my life when this is the way I saw everything. I always looked at women as potential dates (even when I was married to my first wife). I always looked at men as potential threats. Since my experience in life was one of "there is something missing in me," I was always looking through eyes of fear and lack, trying to get others to give me what I thought I was lacking.

There is a wonderful lesson in the workbook of *A Course In Miracles* (number 27) which says, "Above all else, I want to see." I still remember the first time I did that lesson. I thought to myself, "I don't see anyone. All I see are bodies." At this point, I began to practice a new kind of seeing, one in which I would look beyond the person's appearance to his or her soul or essence, to the place inside where we are all the same. I tried to see everyone as my beloved brother or sister, as someone to love rather than as someone to be afraid of or to use.

Dr. Jerry Jampolski, the author of several books including *Love Is Letting Go of Fear* and the founder of the Attitudinal Healing Centers, says that at those centers he would encourage the kids to look for the light in people rather than focusing on the lampshade. These centers are places for children with catastrophic conditions, so there are often kids there whose hair has fallen out from doses of chemotherapy, or who are otherwise disfigured in some way. What a wonderful place to practice seeing the essence, soul, or spirit of everyone. And what a wonderful visual image, to ask ourselves, "Am I looking for the light in him or her, or am I focused on the lampshade?"

Look for a Win-Win

Another way to practice living in the fourth dimension is to practice the principle of win-win in all your transactions, including your financial ones. Most of us are so used to win-lose and competition that it will take a lot of practice (and willingness) to change this habit. Imagine looking to buy an item from someone, and having the thought, "I want you to make a profit as you sell this to me. I want you to win as much as I want me to win." Most of us are so used to the thought, "How little can I pay for this? Am I going to 'take' this person or is he/she going to 'take' me? Which of us is going to get the better of the other?" The inner shift is to "How can we both win in this transaction?"

Practicing win-win everywhere in your life supports you in developing a prosperity consciousness. It also supports you in having an experience of ease in creating what you want in life. Imagine leaving generous tips not only because of what it does for your server but also because of what it does for the state of your prosperity consciousness. Imagine practicing generosity in all your doings not only for what it does for those in your life but for what it does for you.

We are all children of God, and we all deserve to prosper. Furthermore, we deserve to know that our prosperity is based on creation rather than on hard work and suffering. Practice living in the Kingdom of Heaven. Practice living in the realm of conscious experience of oneness with God. Practice living in the fourth dimension. Practice demonstrating and seeing the truth of God's thought system of abundance, beginning with yourself. It is a powerful way to build a prosperity consciousness.

CHAPTER FOUR

Money as an Aspect of God's Love

There is an "old" saying in some "New Thought" circles which goes like this: "There is a Power for good in the universe, and we can learn to use It." The idea is that God is like a big warehouse in the sky, which, if we learn how to tap into It, will provide us with everything we want.

A *newer* way of looking at this idea is to say "There is a Power for wholeness in the universe, and we can so transform ourselves that we experience oneness with It." We can open to It. We can surrender to It. We can cooperate with It. We can align our hearts and minds with It, and we can tune into It. We can even learn that the only true will we have is the same as the one It has for us, and that It's will for us is our certain destiny.

Our Success is Inevitable

One of my favorites among Jesus' parables is the one usually called "The Parable of the Importunate Widow." With a new understanding thanks to Dr. Rocco Errico, the Aramaic Bible scholar, this parable becomes an example of Jesus' teaching on how certain we are to experience success, in the fullest sense of the word.

The essence of the Parable, found in Luke 18, is that there is a certain judge who has no regard for either God or human beings. At a seminar I attended Dr. Errico said that this is a figure of speech meaning he is "on the take" (to use a *current* figure of speech). A widow with a grievance comes before the judge and asks for relief. The judge refuses her request, but the widow won't stop pestering him. Night and day she continues. Finally, he says, "Even though I have no regard for either God or people, yet will I give this widow what she wants to get her to stop pestering me."

The reason this parable is called "The Parable of the Importunate Widow" is because of Matthew's commentary. Matthew says that Jesus gave us this parable "to teach us that we ought always to pray and not to faint." (Luke 18:1) So, according to the way Matthew understands the story, the unjust judge represents God. This is actually a bit ridiculous when we think about it. Why would Jesus portray God as an dishonest judge?

At this same seminar Dr. Errico said that the key to understanding the parable is to realize that all parables, including this one, are about the Kingdom of Heaven (an experience of God's sovereign presence). This, he said, leads us to a second key – to realize that we have had the story backward. It isn't the *judge* who represents God (or the Kingdom of Heaven) but the *widow*. The widow is the Kingdom of Heaven, and we each are the judge. Jesus' message is that, sooner or later, we will have to individually and collectively give up our resistance to God and surrender to oneness with all that God is.

Dr. Errico said that another example of this sentiment is the last part of the beloved Twenty-Third Psalm. The version we have in most Bibles says, "Surely goodness and mercy shall follow me all the days of my life, and I will dwell in the House of the Lord forever." That version is beautiful enough. But in Aramaic, this verse translates more accurately as, "Surely goodness and mercy will haunt me, torment me, dog me, and not leave me alone until I say yes to it."

Accept Your Place in Heaven Sooner

A few years ago, there was a commercial for motor oil which reminded me of this. In the commercial, an auto mechanic told us how much it was to get our oil changed regularly, and how much it cost to have our auto's engine overhauled if we didn't change our oil regularly. He concluded by saying, "So, you can see me now, or you can see me later." What the above parable is saying to all of us is, "You can surrender to God now, or you can surrender to God later. But sooner or later, you will have no choice but to accept the happiness, success, and peace which are your destiny."

At our school, we do a lot of work with people on healing their childhood issues with God. Until such a healing occurs, there is an actual child in us who still thinks that God is a being "up there" somewhere, even if our conscious belief says otherwise. This is why we may still have some fear when we think about "surrendering to God." But there is no being up there sitting on a cloud, judging us, testing us, giving us crosses to bear, or sending some of us to a place called Hell. There is only the energy of Unconditional Love constantly extending Itself to us. This is the destiny to which we eventually must surrender.

Jesus said, "God makes the rain to fall on the just and on the unjust. He makes the sun to shine on the evil and on the good." The word we translate as "evil" can be more accurately translated as "immature." So, to put it another way, God makes the sun to shine on the mature and on the immature. This means that none of the people on whom the sun shines "earn" it by being virtuous or good. It is a gift of God. This is how it is with God's love in all forms, including money. God simply loves us all equally, without regard for how much we think we have earned it.

Many years ago, the young son of a classmate said, "Dad, I think I've got it." His father said, "You think you've got what, son?" His son replied, "I think I understand what the problem is. God keeps pushing our good at us, and we keep pushing it back."

Receiving All That God Has for Us

One of my other favorite parables – a favorite of a great many people – is the one we know as the Parable of the Prodigal Son. You may know the story, but here is a brief recounting of it as found in Luke 15.

A man has two sons. One says to his dad, "Father, give me my inheritance. I want to leave home." His father gives him his inheritance, and he goes off to a "far country," where he "wastes the inheritance in riotous living." A short time later, there is a famine in that country. (There is always a famine in our lives when we are in a far country, when we feel separate from God.) After he has run out of money, the son is destitute, and the only job he can get is that of feeding swine. (He is, of course, Jewish. What an indignity!) The story continues by saying that the farmer for whom he worked wouldn't even let him eat some of the husks he was feeding to the pigs.

Then, the story says, he "comes to himself." He thinks, "What am I doing? Even my father's servants are treated better than this. I will arise, go to my father, and say, 'Father, I don't deserve to be your son. Just make me one of your hired hands.'" As he starts the journey back to his father, the father sees him coming a long way off. He runs to meet him. He covers him with kisses and says to the servants, "Bring a robe, and put it on him. Give him a ring for his finger and sandals for his feet. Let us kill the fatted calf and make merry. My son, who was dead, is alive again."

If you remember the story, all was well at this point except with one person – the older brother. When he hears the commotion, he asks what is going on. When he finds out, he is furious. He says to the dad, "All these years I have served you. You never once offered me so much as the kid of a goat for me and my friends to have a party. But now that this undeserving brother of mine has come back after wasting all his money, you roll out the red carpet."

A great many of us can probably relate to this older brother. The older brother is all of us who have been "dutiful." He represents those of us who have "sacrificed" for the good of others, those of us who have tried to be "good" or "virtuous," and those of us who have worked really hard.

What does the dad say? "Son, you are always with me, and *all that I have is yours.*" The implied phrase which follows is, "and all you have to do is to ask for it." Our prosperity is not the result of working hard, or being good. It is certainly not the result of sacrificing. It is the result of "coming to ourselves" and opening to receive the love which God so freely gives to everyone in all forms, including money.

Healing Your Relationship with Money

Does it surprise you that I would call money a form of God's love? Perhaps, like many of us, you grew up thinking that the words "God" and "money" are mutually exclusive. Perhaps you grew up hearing such things as, "Money is the root of all evil," (which is, of course, an inaccurate fragment of what the Apostle Paul wrote in 1 Tim. 6:10), or "The love of money is the root of all evil" (which is what he actually did write). Perhaps you heard money called "filthy lucre." Perhaps you heard that "You cannot serve God and mammon," and that mammon and money were the same things. Or, you heard, as I mentioned in the story of Jesus and the rich, young ruler, about how hard it is for a rich man to enter the Kingdom of Heaven.

One activity which is essential in building a prosperity consciousness is laying to rest these mistaken ideas. If God is the energy of unconditional love (which is the case), why would this Energy want you to have less money? God (unconditional love) simply wants us all to be equally prosperous, the same way you and I would want all our children to do well. Neither money nor the love of money is the "root of all evil", even if the Apostle Paul did say it. Does the love of money cause people to beat their children or to commit rape? Of course not.

As to the word "evil," the word in Aramaic which we translate as "evil" meant "immature," or "unripe." Dr. Errico says, on page 104 of *Setting a Trap for God*, that if someone in Jesus' day was referring to a green fig on a tree, he would say (if he was speaking English), "That fig is evil." He didn't mean the fig was bad, of course. He simply meant it was not yet ripe. When Jesus said, "Resist not evil," (Mt. 5:39) and, "Sufficient unto today is the evil thereof," (as we have it in Mt. 6:34 in the King James version of the Bible), he was speaking of immaturity, and the problems we face as a result. There simply is no "power of darkness" or "force of evil" anymore than there is a force called "cold" or an actual power called "dark." As we know, cold is simply the absence of heat, and darkness is the absence of light. And there are no "evil" (irretrievably bad) people. We are all made in the image and after the likeness of God.

So the love of money is not the root of all immaturity. Nor is there anything filthy about it. And the phrase "you can't serve God and mammon" means, "You can't experience that God in you is the Source of your success if you also make a cause out of things outside yourself." (The word "cause" is a synonym for "god.") One meaning of the word mammon is "the realm of external, or material, causes. As I think of this meaning, I always remind myself and others, "Money never solves prosperity problems." Only releasing fear and opening to love does that.

What We Learned About Money in Church

Do you remember scenes from church, temple, or synagogue regarding money? How was money talked about by your minister, rabbi, or priest? How did your parents feel about money and spirituality? Did the two go together as far as they were concerned? It is important to heal the issues which the child in us has about money and spirituality because our most deeply-held emotions and decisions are constantly creating our reality, including the ones we have about God and money. You might have even noticed that just reading this material has brought emotions close to the surface.

The minister of my childhood church used to call money "filthy lucre" a lot, and talk about how the love of money is the root of all evil. Yet, I noticed that money was not so filthy or "evil" when it came to what the church needed. When it involved a new roof, a new Sunday School wing, or money to support the missions in Africa, money became a good thing, something to be wanted – even loved. The truth, of course, is that everyone loves money in some way, and it isn't any easier to be spiritual when we are poor than it is when we are rich. It takes constant attention to consistently put God first in our lives. And putting God first is the first principle of true prosperity.

Another seemingly "anti-prosperity" story many of us remember is when Jesus said, "Lay not up for yourselves treasures on earth, where moth and rust can corrupt and thieves can steal. Instead, lay up for yourselves treasures in Heaven... for where your treasure is, there will your heart be also." (Mt. 6:19-21) When I ask the Holy Spirit in me what Jesus meant by these words, I am reminded of his words in the Parable of the Talents. In that story, he has the master say to the servant, "If you were afraid of me, you could have at least put my money in the bank so it would earn interest for me." (Mt. 25:27) The other two servants, of course, doubled their master's money. There is a metaphysical meaning to this story, one which goes far beyond money, but suffice it to say that Jesus was not "anti-savings accounts." What he taught was how to live in the Kingdom of Heaven (by laying up treasures there), how to put God first in every way, how to share what we have, and how to experience life as the feast it was meant to be.

There are basically two ways to save money. We can either save for the vision we have, or we can save because we're afraid.

If we're saving for the possibility of disaster, what usually happens? A rainy day. Because our most deeply-held beliefs and emotions are constantly creating our reality, we get to be right that it was a good thing that we did save for this.

Saving for a vision is another matter altogether. The Bible says, "Without a vision, the people perish." (Prov. 29:18) I am always both living in and enjoying *this* moment and planning for the vision I have of the future. Currently, that vision is for our school to have a retreat center. We have a retreat center fund and a treasure map (see Appendix C to learn how to make a treasure map) for this vision. The vision is there because, when we went within and asked the Holy Spirit what the school is to be, this is what we saw and heard. We fully expect this vision to materialize because we see it so clearly. If, for some reason, it does not, I would not be devastated. I would know that the "something even better" (which is the phrase we have at the bottom of each treasure map we do) is unfolding. Even though I have "treasure" in the bank, my real treasure is in my relationship with God in me. I have always felt supported by the universe and by God in me when I have a vision and save for it.

I think it is important to confront these Bible stories, to look at them and ask what they really mean. Why? Because there is a child in us all who learned very deeply that there is a certain "way things are." One thing many of us learned as children is that money is just not spiritual, and that, if we are spiritual, we will be completely unconcerned about money.

Healing Your Beliefs About Money

How can you heal the relationship your inner child has with money? Here are a few possibilities:

1. Develop a relationship with a spiritual counselor such as a Breath Integration Counselor or Rebirther. Share your issues about money with this counselor and ask for help.

2. Visualize yourself as the child you were somewhere between the ages of three and eight. Ask the child in you what he/she learned about money from his/her parents and religious teachers. Write the answers which come to you with your non-dominant hand.

3. Allow yourself to have the emotions which come up as you do this type of work. See Chapter Seven for more help with this.

4. Write affirmations about how you forgive others for teaching you erroneous concepts about money and about how you forgive yourself for making erroneous decisions. Also, write affirmations regarding the spiritual truth about money. See Appendix A for a list of affirmations from which to choose.

I learned some very powerful lessons about my relationship with money when I became a Breath Integration Counselor. At this point I began to charge a fee for the sessions I offered. Until that time, I had been the minister of churches, and all the counseling and other services I offered were on a free-will offering basis. When I began to offer these breath sessions, however, the guidance I received was to set a price. Relative to what others were charging, it was a very low price, but it was, never-the-less, a set fee. As I told people what I would charge them to have a breath session with me, I had to confront thoughts like, "If I'm doing God's work, I shouldn't charge for it. God's work should be free." When I had that thought, I found myself thinking, "Well then, Phil, just exactly what kinds of work do you think are *not* God's work? Is farming God's work? Is pipe-fitting God's work? Is accounting God's work? Is a hardware store God's work? Do these people receive a set fee or price for what they offer? What makes you think that God's work is so separate from the rest of life?" No wonder I felt guilty about receiving my salary as a minister! It was amazing to me how many thoughts of separation I had regarding spirituality and money.

Following the guidance I received and charging for this "spiritual" work was one of the best learning experiences I ever had. Once I got past the mistaken spiritual ideas on the surface, I then got to have a look at the self-esteem issues which arose about charging a set fee for my services. This, of course, was the real reason my judgments came up so ferociously. Would people still want to work with me if I didn't say they could pay me whatever they wanted? Did I think that time invested with me was valuable?

The Purpose of Money

What is money, anyway? Is it what our ego minds would have us believe – another device to prove that lack and separation from each other are real? Is it really "filthy lucre," "the root of all evil?" Is it something that, if we have too much of it, will keep us out of the Kingdom of Heaven? Do we really have to choose between loving God and loving money?

I love the concept in *A Course In Miracles* which says that the Holy Spirit can reinterpret anything that we have used as a device for separation so that it becomes an instrument to teach love and oneness. The easiest example of this is if we think about our bodies. To my body's eyes, the fact that I have a body is definite proof that I am separate from everyone else. To my body's eyes, I clearly stop at the edge of my skin, and everyone else starts at the edge of theirs. Also, our ego would have us believe that the way to have what we want is to use other people's bodies for pleasure. This, it tells us, will make us happy. It never does, of course. Whenever we attempt to use another person for any reason, we are always left saying, "Is that all there is?"

The Holy Spirit will, if we ask It, will help us to reinterpret our bodies so they become instruments to communicate love and to experience oneness with God and other people. For example, since I have learned how to open to my emotional self, I have had the most profound experiences of oneness – both with God and with other people – in my life, and *in my body*.

The same can be true for money, and it has been so for me. One thing money cannot do is to make us happy. This has been told to us repeatedly by those who have been both rich and poor, even if, as Pearl Bailey said, "Honey, I've been rich and I've been poor, and rich is better." I, too, have been both, and she's right. Rich is definitely better. But it never made me happy. It just made certain things in my life easier. The other thing money can't do, as I said earlier, is to solve prosperity problems. It is almost always impossible to convince anyone of either of these two "can'ts" until they, like me, experience having lots more money than they once did. Then they discover, as I did, that a prosperity consciousness is infinitely more valuable than simply having lots of money.

Give Your Relationship with Money to the Holy Spirit

Since I gave my relationship with money to the Holy Spirit, the Holy Spirit has shown me how to have money become a tool to communicate love, abundance, and oneness rather than being a device to create even more separation among us, and between us and God. For example, as I practice tithing and putting God first in my life, as I practice generosity, as I put money into circulation, as I invest it in the dreams and visions of others, I have the experience that my money is increasingly becoming a tool to support oneness, love, abundance, and spiritual growth.

At prosperity workshops we lead, we often ask people to do the following "sentence completion" exercise: "Money is......" The answers we receive are as varied as the people at the workshops. They are often highly-charged emotionally, as well. I still remember the sentence completion exercise I did at the first prosperity workshop I attended as a student. I was to complete the sentences, "Rich people are...." and "Poor people are....." I found that as I wrote my thoughts about "poor people," I became angrier and angrier. My thought was that, no matter how much I had, I had to give it away if there was anyone who had less than me. Because of how guilty I felt, I couldn't let myself have much money at all. As I worked with this belief, I began to realize that this is not so. Although I am happy to share what I have, I deserve to keep a portion of all I earn. I can be both prosperous *and* one with others. I can give what I give with a feeling of love rather than from a feeling of guilt.

At these workshops, we always finish the "Money is" exercise by asking what money *really* is. The participants always answer, "a means of exchange." This, of course, is what money really is, and it is more than that. As a means of exchange, it is a way to make our lives easier, and it is also a way to unite us. Something you may or may not know about the money we use in the United States is that part of its original purpose was to do just that – to unite us as one country. It helped to bring the thirteen states, which often seemed to have more differences than things in common, together as one unit.

Money also allows us all to specialize and to live our visions. Because of money, I can focus on the things I love to do. I can express my passion, and I can contribute in all the ways I love to contribute. The same is true for you.

At our prosperity workshops, we always tell people that the beginning of healing our relationship with money is to give this relationship to the Holy Spirit. We encourage them to say, just as we ourselves have said, *"I give my relationship with money to the Holy Spirit."* This is a powerful thing to do because the Holy Spirit is the aspect of God which is constantly and gently drawing us upward, toward our wholeness and happiness. At our invitation, the Holy Spirit always changes the goal of the relationship from one which promotes separateness, lack, and fear to one which promotes oneness, abundance, and love.

Learning How to Receive Love

Along with being a means of exchange, money is also something even more profound. It is a form of God's love in our lives.

In our prosperity workshops, we focus on love as much as we do on money. We have found, for example, that a powerful way to receive more money is to open our hearts to receive more love.

In one of the first prosperity workshops Lura and I led together, we were explaining this concept and talking about receiving people's love. One woman, who had apparently signed up to attend this workshop without knowing that it had a spiritual basis, stood up and said, "I don't care about this spiritual stuff, and I don't want to know how to receive people's love. I just want their money." We told her that if she decided to stay, now that she knew more of what we were teaching, she would, indeed, prosper by learning how to receive people's love, as well as how to extend hers to them. She later thanked us for showing her what the subjects of love and money had to do with each other.

Long experience has shown me that we are able to receive God's love in the form of money about as well as we are able to receive God's love in its other forms. For example, God's love in the form of ideas comes to us both from within and from without, both through inner flashes and through the voices of the people in our lives. One of the principles we employ at our staff meetings is called "surrendering to the highest thought." We've gotten used to the idea that the Holy Spirit can speak through anyone, regardless of their position. As soon as we hear what sounds to us like the Holy Spirit speaking, there is shift in our bodies. Something in us resonates to what is being said, and everyone there can feel it.

It takes a certain amount of working on our emotions and on our issues to become sensitive enough to "hear" the highest thought, regardless of where it originates. There was a time in my life when I wasn't open to the idea of hearing guidance, so I couldn't hear it. To this same extent, I also wasn't very open to receiving love in other forms, including the form called "money-making ideas."

Learning How to Receive Support

Another form of God's love is called service, or, as we sometimes call it, "support." To receive support is to allow ourselves to be served by others. Just now, you are being served or supported by me, as you read this book. The easier it is for you to receive my love in this form, the more it will benefit you. We all receive service from each other in a variety of ways (thanks, in part, to money). In fact, one of the prosperity principles we teach is for us to do the things we love to do, and to be willing to pay others to do those things we don't love to do. For example, I'm very glad that there are people who love to do accounting and others who love to work on cars. I don't like to do either of those things, and I am very glad to pay people who do.

One application of this principle of receiving support is to be open to mental, emotional, and spiritual support. I've spent the past twenty or so years offering counseling sessions. These are more like coaching sessions than therapy sessions, but thank God we live in a time when we can go to see someone for support without the stigma of "he must be crazy if he is seeing a counselor." These days, it is not seen so much as an admission of weakness to have a coach or counselor as it is an expression of high self-esteem. I think one thing this means is that it is getting easier for us to acknowledge God in us as our constant counselor.

Yet another form of God's love is affection. Babies need a certain amount of affection in order to survive. Actually, so do adults. This can be in the form of hugs, caresses, or the expression of our sexuality. The ability to easily give and receive affection is a sign of having an openness to God's love in all forms

As we learn to receive all these forms of God's love, our lives become easier and easier, more and more prosperous. The more we learn to be open to any of these forms, the easier it becomes for us to receive all of them, including money.

Loving God and Loving Money

In my life, I practice knowing and loving God as my one Source for everything I want. Knowing God and experiencing oneness with God – this is my greatest treasure. It always comes first. I believe that everyone deserves to experience oneness with God, to have the security and comfort which comes from knowing God as their unlimited Source.

I love God as my Source, and I also love money as a resource. I love God as my one Cause, and I love the effect in my life called money. I find no conflict here at all. I serve God, and I let money serve me. I also find that as I let myself love both God and money, I tend to have more of both in my life. This is because of a spiritual law which says, "Whatever we love expands."

As we follow the evolution of money, we see that it began as a valuable metal (such as gold or silver) which could be traded. These pieces of metal took the place of trading actual goods. Then the pieces metal became pieces of paper which *represented* those metals. The metals themselves were stored in government vaults. Then money became pieces of paper *without* precious metals backing them up, only the reputation of governments. At the same time, it became other pieces of paper (checks), representing the "money" each of us had put into a bank account. Then it became pieces of plastic, also representing these accounts with "money" in them at our banks. Then it became simply the *numbers* from those pieces of plastic as "money" is transferred electronically.

The Properties of Money

What started out as a concrete "thing" has become, increasingly, an idea. It was always an idea, of course, even when it looked more concrete. It is the idea of trading goods and services. Just as each of us is an idea in the mind of God, so money is an idea in our collective mind. And, as I said in the last chapter, ideas have certain properties. For example, they are not diminished by sharing or giving, just like love isn't diminished by sharing or giving. Rather, they grow and become more real as they are shared and expressed.

The particular idea called money has a couple of other properties worth noting. One of them is that money is facility, not reward. Having enough money facilitates having the kind of life we want to have, and it facilitates us in expressing our gifts in the ways we want to express them. For example, it allows us to refresh and recreate ourselves so we can more effectively give. It is not, however, a "reward."

So many of us learned, as children, that money was what we received when we were "good," or when we did our chores well. So, even as adults, we tend to think of money in that same way. "If only I am good enough or virtuous enough," we think, "I'll have the money and life I want." This is a concept that has left many spiritually-based people disappointed. Having been "good" for so many years, they can't understand why they aren't more prosperous. But there is no relationship between being virtuous and being prosperous. There *is*, however, a relationship between opening to God's love (in all its forms) and having the prosperity we want and deserve.

Another property of the idea called money is that it is, like time, actually elastic. If we view money only as a "particle" and not as a "wave," it seems to be finite. We can, of course, view time in the same way. But have you ever noticed how time seems to expand and contract depending on your frame of mind and emotion? Money has the same property. The same amount of money will go further or less far depending on our state of consciousness.

The time in my life when I noticed this the most was when I began to tithe. After giving ten-percent to God in me, and then giving it to wherever God in me directed, I should have had ten-percent less money with which to pay my bills. I should have had, according to my logical, "left brain" mind, ninety percent of the lifestyle I had had before I began to tithe. Except this wasn't my experience. Sometimes I seemed to have about the same amount of money as I had had before I began to tithe, but most of the time I had more. I never did have the experience of having less. When I am in tune with God in me, when I am "in the zone," the money I have seems to go a great deal further than when I am in a consciousness of lack. The more I open to God's love, the more my experience of "God's love in the form of money" grows.

A Money Problem? No, a Receiving Problem

An old adage says, "Nobody has a money problem. It's always an idea problem." What this means, of course, is that if we are creative enough, there is always a way to have enough money to meet our needs and wants. This thought is a good one in and of itself. But it gets even better when we think of money as having, like us, properties of being both a particle and a wave. Then we could say, "None of us really has a money problem. What we have is a problem of being stuck in the ego's thought system, stuck in seeing money as a thing, and not as an idea." Another version of this thought is to say, "None of us has a money problem. What we have is a receiving problem." This means that there is an apparent lack of money because we have a heart which, at present, is closed to love. This is, however, a condition which we can change.

I was once the minister of a Unity church in Florida. When I arrived at this church, it had more expenses than monthly income. When I left, over four years later, it still had more expenses than monthly income. In the meantime, we had received an inheritance and built a beautiful new church. Our congregation had more than doubled. The other members of the Board of Directors and I had communicated regularly with the congregation about this, and still the situation didn't change.

I used to regularly feel angry about this and have thoughts like, "Don't the people of this church want to give to it? Don't they care?" Of course, beneath these thoughts was guilt about what kind of leader I was. It wasn't until a few years later, as I began my journey of personal transformation, when I realized that my ability to receive was a part of this equation. At that point in my life, my heart was nearly completely closed to receiving love.

Over the past several years, I have come to realize that people absolutely love to give. Sure, there are a few people who are afraid to give, and there are a few people who express their anger by withholding love. By and large though, people love to give. They love to contribute to something greater than themselves. The question is whether there are people and organizations who are capable of receiving their love. At that point in my life, I was not. One of my thoughts which indicated this was, "If you want something done right, do it yourself." This attitude is definitely a symptom of the fear of receiving.

To Receive Is to Surrender

In the work we do at our school, we see this fear of receiving over and over. In fact, it is one of the biggest fears we all have. One reason this seems to be so is that receiving love calls for us to be "out of control." It calls on us to drop our defenses. It calls for us to "surrender." John Denver once sang of a place where "the joy of surrender will bind us." When we learn how safe it is to surrender to love, it really is a joyful experience.

Once, in a Sunday talk, I asked people to do an exercise with me. I asked them to pretend that we were all on the spaceship Enterprise with Captain Kirk. The Klingons are about to attack the vessel (or "wessel" as Chekhov would say). So Captain Kirk gives the command to Mr. Sulu, "Shields up, Mr. Sulu." I then asked them all to imagine a shield going up around them, and to feel how that felt in their bodies. (You could do the same right now if you want.) Then I asked them to imagine that the danger had completely passed, and that Captain Kirk had given the "shields down" command to Mr. Sulu. I then asked the audience to feel how that felt in their bodies. (You can do likewise if you previously put up your own shields). Afterward, a woman came up to me and said, "I got really angry with you in that exercise because

I became aware that my shields were already up. I think they probably are up all the time, and that exercise made me look at that." She later thanked me for showing her that she had another choice.

As I will discuss more fully in chapters six and seven, the only way it makes sense to surrender, to be open and vulnerable, is if we know how powerful we are, if we understand that there is really never anything "out there" except our own mind being reflected back to us. It also wouldn't make sense to practice openness and surrender if there really was a force of evil, a power of darkness. If this were the case, who knows what could happen to us if we practiced defenselessness? It would be better to always have our guard up, to be constantly on the alert. And this is how most of us learned to live – defensively.

As *A Course In Miracles* reminds us, "If I defend myself, I am attacked." (W. p. 252) It also says, "In my defenselessness my safety lies," (W. p. 284) and "All defenses do what they would defend." (T. p. 359) In other words, our defensiveness *produces* the very result we wanted it to protect us from having. There is no such thing as a "force of evil." There is only maturity and immaturity, love and fear. The more we know that, the safer it is to open our hearts and surrender to love. The more open we are, the more love – and money – we can receive.

Releasing the Barriers to Receiving

There are several reasons as to why we are afraid to surrender to love. One is that love actually does bring up anything inside us which is unlike it. The way we say it at our school is this: *"Whenever we affirm, experience, claim, receive, or express any of the qualities of God, it brings to the surface any beliefs or emotions which are unlike it so they can be released."*

This includes some seemingly powerful emotions, such as anger, guilt, fear, sadness, and "weak and helpless" feelings. Most of us have spent the better part of our lives trying to keep a lid on these emotions, as well as on thoughts and impulses which, we think, make us unlovable. Take guilt, for example. (To which many people would probably reply, "Yes, please. Take it.") Guilt is the one emotion we would all like most to avoid. As soon as it begins to surface, we do whatever we have to do to get it to stop. We sacrifice again, we hurt ourselves, or we shut down our receiving.

One thing I found to be an absolute must if I wanted to transform my life was that I had to release my attachment to comfort. I had to stop defining whether or not I was being success-ful by whether or not I was comfortable. In other words, I had to keep going past my comfort zone. For a while, I also had to stop using the measure of whether I was "centered" as a criteria of whether or not I was on the right path. As I opened my heart to receive love, I most definitely did not feel centered. And it was not comfortable. It brought feelings to the surface which I had tried for decades to keep suppressed. It also brought to the surface more aliveness than I would have thought possible. And I began to be much more open to receive love in all forms, including money.

Another reason we are so afraid to receive too much love is what we decided that love was when we were children. Remem-ber, there is an actual child in us which is still driving, as far as the really important issues in our lives are concerned.

For example, many of us learned that love and disapproval are the same thing. For us, the way our parents expressed love was to constantly tell us what we were doing wrong. Others of us learned that love and control are the same thing. One or both of our parents expressed their "love" toward us by seeming to want to control how we acted, spoke, felt, and thought. Still others learned that love and punishment are the same thing, or even that love and abuse are the same thing. ("I'm only hurting you like this because I love you"..."This hurts me more than it hurts you.") Then again, some of us learned that love and sacrifice are the same thing. Our parents may have said such things as, "I'm doing without so you can have the things you want or need." Imagine the resistance we will have to receiving love and money if this was the case. Imagine how much guilt it would bring to the surface. Imagine how hard we would try to suppress the guilt.

One very large "how to" about having more money in your life is to simply allow yourself to have as much love – in all forms – as you want. Allow yourself to receive it, and allow yourself to fully express it. Let it flow through your heart as much as you want. As you do this, practice letting it be OK if feelings come to the surface, including guilt. Practice not judging how you feel. One principle practiced in Zen Buddhism is that, no matter what we are experiencing, we can simply "open softly to it." This is especially important with emotions which are very frightening (especially to the child in us) – anger, fear, sadness, guilt, sexual feelings, even aliveness and strength.

Opening to Love by Expressing It

Also, practice letting yourself express as much love as you want to express. Love is one of those things where it is easy to see its "wave-like" quality. The more you express, the more there is to express. The more you express, the more you have. With love, there is never "only so much to go around."

Lura and I practice this in our marriage. We practice that our love for each other is not "special" (to use a term from *A Course In Miracles*). We express love everywhere we can. That doesn't mean we *express* it in all the ways we do with each other, but the *quality* of love we express to everyone is the same. The more Lura expresses love to others, the more there is for me, and the more I express love to others, the more there is for her. We express love to a lot of people. Our goal is to love everyone we meet, because we deserve to experience oneness with God all the time.

It hurts to withhold love – from *anyone*. The only way we can *not* express love to everyone is to suppress the love in us. What I practice in my life is to love everyone, not because *they* deserve to receive it (which, of course, they do) but because *I* deserve to express it. This is one of the very most powerful ways there is to practice accepting our oneness with God. All God does is extend love – everywhere, all the time. God doesn't withhold it from anyone. Sometimes I find it amazing that we put up so many barriers to doing what we want most to do, what comes most naturally – simply giving and receiving love with everyone in our lives.

There is an often-used illustration of what happens when there is not outlet for something. That illustration is a picture of the Dead Sea, on the border of Israel and Syria. Because there is no outlet, the salinity is very high, and because of this high salinity, absolutely nothing lives or grows in this body of water. As Ralph Waldo Emerson said, "Man is the inlet, and may become the outlet, of all there is in God." If we don't express it, we stop the flow. If we do, it is how we experience oneness with God. It is also a powerful way to expand our prosperity consciousness.

Are there times in your life when you particularly notice yourself shutting down your heart, your willingness to extend love? I used to do this all the time in the presence of beggars or panhandlers. Then I began to practice keeping my heart open and feeling my oneness with them. I now simply listen to the Holy Spirit in their presence. I ask, "Am I guided to give money to this person or not? Would such a gift support me and this person, or not?" Whatever the answer, I can keep my heart open. It's just one more opportunity to experience oneness with God.

Our thoughts are constantly creating our reality. Generosity with all forms of love is a sign of an abundant consciousness. The more we practice generosity, the more we will have the means with which to be generous.

Jesus' Teachings About Prosperity

As I look back on the life and teachings of Jesus Christ, I don't find someone who was opposed to prosperity or in favor of poverty. On the contrary, I find someone who said such things as, "I have come that you might have life, and that you might have it abundantly." (Jn. 10:10) "Hitherto, you have asked little in my name. Ask, and you shall receive, that your joy may be full." (Jn. 16:24) "It is your Father's good pleasure to give you the Kingdom." (Lk. 12:32) And, to the older brother of the Prodigal Son, "Son, you are ever with me, and all that I have is yours." (Lk. 15:31)

Jesus, comparing himself to John the Baptist, said, "John came neither eating nor drinking, and people say, 'He is possessed.' I came, both eating and drinking, and people say, 'Look, a glutton and a drunkard, a friend of tax collectors and sinners.' Yet wisdom is justified by her deeds." (Mt. 11:18,19) His first miracle was to prolong a party when he turned water into wine at a wedding feast. Does all this sound like someone teaching us that prosperity is a bad thing? Not at all. What Jesus constantly taught was to keep our priorities straight and to remember what will make us truly happy. "Seek first the Kingdom of Heaven," (an experience of oneness with God) he said, "and all these things will be yours as well." This is not a teaching about how to be "good." It is a teaching about how to be happy, prosperous, and at peace.

CHAPTER FIVE

Resources Follow Commitment

What are your dreams for a better life? Which dreams would you have if you didn't have to know in advance how you were going to actualize them? What lives in your heart as a vision for the kind of person you want to be? For how you want to express yourself in the world? For the quality of life you want?

When I lived in Hawaii, one of my friends used to say, quoting Langston Hughes, *"Hold fast to dreams, for if dreams die, life is a broken winged bird which cannot fly."* This friend was in Hawaii temporarily, taking a break from sailing around the world in his thirty-one foot boat. That was his dream, or one of them, anyway.

As I write this, Lura and I are seven years into a twenty year vision. We wanted to have a school to teach and train ministers who have undergone their own personal transformation. We wanted to have a campus in a city (Minneapolis) and a retreat center in the country. Just before we moved to Minneapolis, while we were living in Taos, New Mexico, we made a "treasure map" (There are instructions for how to construct a treasure map in Appendix C) of what we wanted as part of this vision. As we made this pictured prayer, we said to ourselves, "What if we had twenty years to accomplish all we put on this map? What if we didn't have to know *how* our lives would include all the things pictured? So many things on that pictured prayer have already happened, and I have no doubt that everything else we put on it will show up as well.

For several years, we had this treasure map on one wall of our first classroom in Minneapolis. As our students would look at it, they would see items on the map which had become part of the school, and say, "Look, this item is on the map." I laugh now when I see that one of the items we put on the treasure map was "a real computer." (I was a little slow to join the computer generation.) Now we have several of them.

Let Your Reach Exceed Your Grasp

What does your life look like now? What do you want it to look like in ten years? In twenty? Do you dare to have dreams which go beyond your grasp, beyond your knowledge of how they will happen?

Resources follow commitment. This is a very, very large idea contained within three words. Most of us want it to be the other way around. We want to see the resources first before we commit to having something. We especially wouldn't want anyone else to know about it if we have a vision and don't know how it will actualize. We don't want to look like fools.

We can even hear advice from some quarters which says, "Don't share your dreams out loud. It dissipates the energy." No it doesn't, unless you just share wishes which you have no intention of manifesting, or unless you would rather *talk* about what you want than to work toward having it. If you have friends who are on your side, sharing your dreams with them actually empowers these visions.

Perhaps you are familiar with the following famous advice given by the leader of the Scottish Himalayan expedition, W. H. Murray. This is one of my favorite quotations, and it has been a guiding force in my life for the past twenty-five years:

"Until one is committed, there is hesitancy, the chance to draw back, always ineffectiveness. Concerning all acts of initiative and creation, there is one elementary truth, the ignorance of which kills countless ideas and splendid plans: that the moment one definitely commits oneself, then Providence moves also. All sorts of things occur to help one that would otherwise never have occurred. A whole stream of events issues from the decision, raising in one's favor all manner of unforeseen incidents and meetings and material assistance which no one could have dreamt would have come his way. I have learned a deep respect for one of Goethe's couplets: 'Whatever you can do, or dream you can, begin it. Boldness has genius, power, and magic in it.'"

As I said, this concept is one which I have had to demonstrate in my life again and again. And, no matter how many times I see it work, there is a part of my mind which wants it to be the other way around - - first give me the resources, then I'll commit. I remind myself whenever I'm faced with yet another "upleveling" in my life, "It's safe to commit to this desire. It's safe to commit to having more of what I want."

My First Experience of "Committing First"

The first time I was conscious of needing to demonstrate the truth of this idea was after I heard my guidance say, "You are going to be a minister." The commitment I had to make at that point was to say "yes" to this guidance, even though I didn't know what it meant. The church I was attending had no seminary. I didn't know where I would go to school, nor was there a religious path which called to me at the time. However, the experience was so real, it never really occurred to me to say no to it. A few years later, I discovered the local Unity church, and I found out that they had a ministerial school just outside Kansas City, Missouri. I joined the Unity church in Minneapolis, and a short time later applied to become a student at Unity Village.

At that time, my wife and I were deeply in debt. Also, I had no idea how I would pay for my ministerial education. I still remember my local Unity Minister saying to me, "Phil, when God has a plan, God pays the expenses." It sounded like a wonderful thought. Not that I understood it fully. I even briefly had the thought that if God was going to pay the expenses, I didn't have to do anything. I could simply wait for God to put the money into my account. It didn't take long to realize (as you also do if you've ever tried this plan) that this isn't how it works.

What did happen, however, is that opportunities began to present themselves. At this time, I worked in a small carpet store, selling carpet and helping to install it. The man I worked for also had a dream. He wanted to move his family to Jackson, Wyoming. We had a deal: Whichever of us first found a way to actualize our dream, the other would be supportive.

So, with the support of my wife and my boss, I applied to Unity's ministerial school and went for interviews at Unity Village. I was accepted as a student in the next year's class! Now, how to pay for it. The first step was to get out of debt so we could be debt-free as we arrived in Kansas City. My boss began to give me the easy installation jobs, ones I could do in evening hours. With his support, and that of my first wife, Marilyn, we were able to leave Minneapolis debt-free. Had I not had a vision and said "yes" to it, it's easy to imagine still being deeply in debt, twenty-five years later.

There was at least one other aspect of this "resources follow commitment" principle I needed to face. As we were driving to Kansas City to begin my studies, I had the thought, "Maybe there is a course of study at this school which would lead to my being a 'counseling minister,' one who doesn't have to do public speaking." (I was terrified to do public speaking). What I discovered was that everyone in my class took the same courses, and that one of only two courses offered during my entire ministerial course of study was speech. How grateful I now am that I said yes to this vision, even though I was so afraid. Public speaking is now one of my passions, something I've loved to do ever since I got through my initial fears.

When I graduated from ministerial school, my first church was in Florida, where I had another experience of resources following commitment. We began construction of a $350,000 church building without having all the money in place to finish it. When I asked the Holy Spirit if this was the right thing to do, I heard a resounding "yes." We went ahead, and everything fell into place.

The Coin in the Mouth of the Fish

One of the stories in the Gospels tells of Jesus' disciples coming to him and saying, "Master, we need to pay a tax." Jesus said to them, "Go to a certain place, and there you will find a fish with a coin in its mouth." (Mt. 17:27) To some people, this is an example of Jesus performing a miracle. However, according to Dr. Rocco Errico, the phrase "something with a coin in its mouth" is an Aramaic figure of speech. When Jesus told his disciples they would find a fish with a coin in its mouth, he meant, "Some of you know how to fish commercially. This is what you did for a living. Go, catch some fish, and use the proceeds to pay the tax."

There is also a metaphysical meaning to this story. In the Bible, fish often represent ideas. Also metaphysically, a tax represents the requirements of life. So one meaning of this story is that whenever we have an idea, the means to actualize it will also be presented.

After being the minister of Unity of New Port Richey for over four years, my next ministry was in Hawaii. It was here that my personal and spiritual growth would accelerate dramatically. For over a year before I made this move, I had been a member of a prayer group in Florida. Weekly we met and affirmed the steps of

"The Master Mind Principle," the prayer program created by the Reverend Jack Boland. One of those steps says, "I ask to be changed at depth." I certainly received a powerful answer to that prayer.

Looking back, I have often marveled at the workings of the Holy Spirit – picking my wife and I up and moving us 5,000 miles to the perfect place to begin my process of deep personal transformation. The *stated* reasons for bringing me to Hawaii were to supervise the renovation of the buildings at the Unity Church of Hawaii, and to begin a new Unity church on the Windward side of the island. Both of those things happened, but they were not the major reason I was there. I was there to participate in my own healing, to be "changed at depth."

Shortly after moving to Hawaii, the Senior Minister and I visited a large Religious Science church in San Diego and had lunch with its minister, The Rev. Terry Cole-Whittaker. At lunch, I did something I had done with several other successful ministers. I asked her the question, "Terry, to what do you attribute your remarkable success? (At this time, her church had some 3,500 people attending each Sunday.) I fully expected her to talk about the *est training* and its related programs. At that time, Terry was a well-known promoter of what is now called *The Forum*. Surprisingly, she started talking about something called "Rebirthing." She told me of some Rebirthing sessions she had had and said it was the best thing she had ever done to remove inner barriers to success. I thought to myself, "I know the man she had these sessions with. He now lives in Hawaii, and I just heard him speak last week. I think I'll have lunch with him."

My Deep Transformation Begins

As a result of the lunch I had with the Rebirther, I was invited to attend a relationships workshop. At this workshop, there was a point where the leaders were discussing birth trauma. They said it was often a source of decisions that affect us our entire lives. Then they began to talk about the kind of birth which many people my age would have experienced.

For example, we would probably have been treated pretty much like a lump of clay, because they didn't then know that newborns have feelings in the same way that older children do. We would probably have had our umbilical cords cut before we had had a chance to expel the amniotic fluid from our lungs. This would have resulted in us having the experience that we couldn't get any air. It would have felt the same as if we had been drowning, so we would have been terrified. We then would have been slapped to get us breathing. This scenario would reflect a "normal" birth, one without "complications."

All this would have resulted in us making a number of decisions, such as, "It's a struggle to get what I want in life," and "There's not enough for me." As this material was being presented, I was sitting in the body of the workshop simply listening. As I did, I began to have the sensation that my legs were made of rubber, and I felt like an elephant was sitting on my chest. I doubt that I could have arisen from my chair and walked right then. I thought to myself, "Hmm. I think there is something about this that I need to explore."

With this in mind, I scheduled a Rebirthing session. I didn't know what these were, but I thought one was all that would be needed. "Once I had been rebirthed," I thought, "why would I need to be rebirthed again?" But it turned out that Rebirthing is a form of deep, oral breathing which one does, with support from a Rebirther, for about an hour. These sessions are usually done in a series of weekly sessions, so I scheduled such a series. I never experienced anything so powerful in my life! Things which I did not believe were possible to change began to change. I actually began to transform in relation to who I thought I was.

At some point during this series, I heard about a six-month-long program of personal transformation. When I asked my Rebirther about it, he replied that he could see me in this program.

That wasn't what I had asked, so I then got very defensive and judgmental. I told him that the tuition for this course, which at the time was $5,200, "was a lot of money as far as I was concerned." I went on to say that I didn't have that kind of money, and what did he tell people when they told him that they couldn't afford it?

He said that if someone told him they wanted something – a six-month program, a car, or anything else – and that they couldn't afford it, he thought that his job as a spiritual teacher was to not believe them. I still remember how much the truth of that answer resonated in me. Later, with my curiosity now really piqued about this program. I said, "My thought about this program is that if the Holy Spirit wants me to this program, the Holy Spirit will put $5,200 in my bank account."

A Deeper Level of Asking

His response was that if I was going to wait to commit to doing the program until the money was in the bank, I would probably be waiting a long time. At this point in my life, I began to learn about a deeper level of asking – that we are always receiving what we are asking for, if we understand what it really means to ask. In other words, we are always receiving the results of our deepest thoughts and feelings. If we do nothing different, our lives will continue to unfold pretty much as they have been unfolding. What we will have in our lives and in our bank accounts is what was there yesterday. The only way our lives are going to change is if we do something different, take some action, make a commitment first.

In my ministerial life, I would call this "putting legs on our prayers" – not only saying what we want but taking action to support its creation. In other words, if we commit first, start placing the weight of our consciousness on what we *want* to be true instead of what we *don't want* to be true, our world will begin to change. We are, in taking action, "asking" in a much more powerful way than if we were asking with words alone.

I was invited to go to a support meeting about this program, so I went, thinking, "I'll just go to see what it's like." At the meeting, everyone shared about what they wanted to receive from being there. When it was my turn, I was asked if this program looked like something I wanted to do. I replied, "Well, yes it is. I'd like to do the program, but ..." I was all set to go into what I *really* wanted to say, which was a list of reasons why I couldn't do it. Instead, the leader asked me to stop there for a moment. He said he knew I had considerations about doing this, but before I shared them, would I mind saying that first part again, just by itself? The part about wanting to do the program?

Now I really felt exposed. I started to get physically hot. I felt as though someone was asking me to take responsibility for saying what I wanted. This was something I hardly ever did. If someone asked, "Where would you like to go to lunch," my normal response was to say, "I don't know. Where do you want to go?" The person would say something like, "I feel like a hamburger today. Let's go to McDonald's." I'd say, "Fine with me," and then I would secretly resent him or her for actually saying what he or she wanted when I believed I couldn't so that.

So for me to take responsibility for saying what I wanted felt very confrontive. But I did say it again, and, as I did, it really resonated in my body as the truth. Then, as I shared my considerations, the leader responded to them in a way that felt right to me. As he spoke, I thought again, "You know, this really *is* something I want to do. I'm just scared because I don't have a clue about where I would get the tuition."

Receiving Support in Having What I Wanted

I shared this with the leader, who replied that he didn't think I had any difficulty with manifestation. He thought my problem was how much I held myself back. He said he had an idea, something he thought would support me in creating the money for the program. If I really wanted to do this program, I could write out a $500 check right now which would be a non-refundable deposit." I said, "I don't have enough money in my account for you to cash it." He said not to worry, that he wouldn't cash it until I told him it was good. Writing the check was simply a way for me to declare to the universe that this was something I intended to do.

I wrote the check, thinking to myself, "This will never work." But three days later, I got a call from the church administrator saying, "Someone just brought to my attention that you've got several hundred dollars worth of royalties coming to you from the church. This money is for cassette tape albums of yours which we've sold." I asked her how much it was. She said it was about $420. This meant that my check could be cashed! I was amazed.

I attended the next support meeting and said, "It worked! You can cash the check!" The leader congratulated me and asked if I wanted to try it again. This time, he said, I could write a check for the balance, for $4,700. As I took out my checkbook and began to write the check, my hand was shaking so much I could hardly write. I had never given myself a gift anywhere *close* to this size. As I thought back on my life, I thought, "I could raise $350,000 to build a church building. I could begin a new church in Hawaii from scratch and have two-hundred people attending it from the first Sunday. I could manifest a lot of things in my life, *as long as they weren't this personal*." The idea of doing something like this just to improve the quality of my life was nearly incomprehensible.

After I had written the check, I built up a few hundred dollars in a fund I had begun. Meanwhile, I had received a list of affirmations I could write about creating the tuition. I wrote lots of affirmations, especially ones about how "God in me is the unlimited Source of everything I want in life, including money." As I thought about how I would manifest this money, I realized that this concept – that God is the Source of my money – was just a "good idea" in my life, not something I actually experienced on a daily basis. I had been teaching it for years. I was only now beginning to really look at it, to try to "get it" on a deep level.

Then one day in the mail, I received a notice about a pension fund into which I had been paying. I thought to myself, "If I don't do something to change my life, I won't make it to the age where I could use this money." The notice said I had $6,200 in this fund. I thought, "Eureka! I found my money for this tuition!" I called them up and told them I wanted my money. The man on the other end of the telephone told me I couldn't have it. "Why not?" I asked. "Because," he said, "the agreement you signed says that you can't take this money out until either you turn seventy or until you leave the Unity Movement."

What it Means to Be Fully Committed

One minute I was on cloud nine, and the next I was in the depths. Then it occurred to me that this was actually progress. Whereas yesterday I had no idea at all of where I would come up with this kind of money, here was at least *one* place where it existed, even if I couldn't access it. I remember walking out of my office and saying to my secretary, "I am just flat going to do this program. Now I am committed, and I will do whatever it takes to do it." As I said this, I realized that, until just then, I hadn't been fully committed.

I had made a "brainstorming" list of "one way I could create the money for this program." The list included (gulp) talking to my family and friends about a loan. I had been raised to believe that this was not a suitable subject to discuss. In my family, we didn't talk about money, and we certainly didn't ask each other for any kind of financial support. I realized I was even willing to broach this subject, difficult as it seemed to me. I began with the one who was the scariest, my oldest brother. He didn't have any money he could free up, but he actually thanked me for thinking of him. I was stunned. Talk about being wrong about my perceptions! I asked some other people for loans, including some friends. I received no money from any of them, but I felt closer to everyone I asked.

The next thing on my list was even more confrontive. The item on the brainstorming list simply said, "Ask my church." At the next meeting of the Board of Directors, I proposed that they give me $1,000 as a scholarship, and that they loan me $3,200, to be paid back over the next several months from money which they otherwise would be putting into my pension fund. With no hesitation, they said yes, and the treasurer simply wrote me a check. Again, I was stunned. Again, I was wrong about my perception that people didn't want to support me in doing what I wanted to do. As I sat at home later that evening looking at the check, I felt more powerful than I could ever remember feeling. I thought to myself, "If I can do this, I believe I can do anything."

As the program progressed, I received far more than my money's worth from it, many things that completely changed my life for the better. However, nothing I learned while I was actually *in* the program was any bigger than what I learned from the process of creating the money for it – that I can say "yes" to having what I want in life. I can even fully commit to it, even if I have no idea of how it will happen or where the resources will come from to actualize it.

It's Safe to Know What You Want

Many of us actually believe we don't know what we want. However, that is just not true. Somewhere inside us, we all know what we want. Some of us are *afraid* to know because we think it won't do us any good, anyway. Some of us, in childhood, were convinced by others that we didn't know when we actually did. Some of us were taught not to listen to our desires, and/or to not trust what we hear. We were taught that there are rules to follow, rules which preclude us from knowing what we want. Some of us even were taught that what we said we wanted wasn't what we actually did want. "I want ice cream." "No you don't." "I don't?" "No, you want Jell-O, because Jell-O is what we have."

Here is a simple affirmation which I often include when I teach classes on prosperity principles: *"I always know what I want."* In these classes, I sometimes have people pair up with a partner and say this affirmation emphasizing a different word each time. You might want to try this, and to simply notice your thoughts and feelings as you do.

> *I* always know what I want.
> I *always* know what I want.
> I always *know* what I want.
> I always know *what* I want.
> I always know what *I* want.
> I always know what I *want*.

There is a companion sentence which can be done in the same way: *"I can have what I want."* You may also want to write either or both of these powerful affirmations. They actually are the truth, even if they are not yet your experience.

Another reason many of us believe we mustn't know what we want is because we learned that to be in a relationship means to sacrifice. Most of us learned that the way to be "good" people is to put others before ourselves. Thus, we believe that asking for what we want means that someone else is going to lose. Another thought which many of us grew up with is that "nice" or "good" people don't ask. Therefore, if we do ask, this makes us a "bad" (read "unlovable") person. We even might have had the experience that if we asked for something, the love from one or both of our parents got taken away. This, again, leads us to suppress the knowledge of what we want.

If I asked you to list the ten or twenty goals which are the most important to you right now, you might very well include in that list some goals you "should" have, things which others have said you would include if you were any kind of person at all. It's always easy to tell if the goals you write down are your goals. Do you give them priority in your life or not? The ones to which you give priority are your *actual* personal goals.

We can trust ourselves to know what we want if we stop judging our desires. None of us is really going to run off to the south seas to live our lives – unless that really *is* what we want to do with our lives, and we are willing to be responsible for that lifestyle choice. Sometimes in our work we say to our students, "It's safe to know what you want. You can actually trust yourself that much." What we always find is that one desire leads to the next. It is just as possible to find the route to Heaven by knowing our desires and asking for them as it is get there by denying and/or suppressing them.

Release Your Belief in Sacrifice

When Lura and I founded the Unity Church of Clear Lake in southeast Houston, Texas, we incorporated into it a volunteer system we had learned from being part of a transformational community in Vancouver, Canada. One thing we did in this volunteer system was to insist that before people could volunteer, they had to come to an orientation meeting. This, by the way, had an interesting effect. It was almost like using reverse psychology. People thought, "Wow. Volunteering here must really be something if I can't volunteer without attending a meeting first." We *wanted* volunteering at our church to be "really something." One thing we were trying to accomplish was to take the experience of "sacrifice" out of our volunteer activities.

At this meeting we would say, "Think about an area of the church in which you think you want to work. However, before we get to the point of assigning jobs, we want to first take time to focus on you." We would then ask people to write out their personal goals, all the ways they wanted their lives to improve over the next year or so. Did they want improved relationships? Better health? More money? A vacation on a cruise ship? Inner peace? A new car? Whatever their personal desires were, we asked them to write them down, without being concerned if the desires seemed to have anything to do with volunteering at the church. This helped us to help them achieve their goals. As they shared the list with us, we could match them with a volunteer position where they could grow in ways which would help them have what they wanted in life. Then, too, sharing these lists out loud in front of the rest of us was like sharing a prayer request. It helped to make it more real – to us and to the one sharing.

The story which always comes to mind about this is one which also feels like one of our most satisfying successes. An accountant named Floyd came to a meeting thinking he should volunteer to help with the accounting because that was his area of expertise. His list of goals, however, all had to do with wanting more friends. He spoke English as a second language, and he found that this barrier resulted in him becoming very shy and withdrawn. At this same meeting was a woman named Iris who had more people skills than accounting skills. Her big goal was to begin her own bookkeeping service. On the surface, it appeared that the best way to staff the church would be to have Floyd work on the books, and to have Iris be a greeter, or some such position where she could use her people skills. This, however, would not have resulted in committed or dedicated volunteers. It would also not have been teaching ourselves what we wanted to learn – that *we also* were more important than our jobs.

We suggested to Floyd that he be a greeter, letting people know as they arrived at church where they could find child care, Sunday School, or the church service itself in the ballroom. His vocabulary didn't get in the way of sharing a warm smile or giving directions, and he loved his job. He met lots of people and gradually began to form friendships with some of them. Iris became our volunteer bookkeeper. At first, I found this to be a challenging situation, because I sometimes knew more about accounting than she did. However, she also loved her position, and she did learn. This experience supported her in eventually opening a bookkeeping service. As she went to school to learn the principles and skills she would need, she had the church as a "practice exercise." As a result, the church also won because she, too, was a fiercely loyal volunteer.

With some people, it was difficult to get across the idea that a personal goal was something which would directly improve their lives. Some people would write goals like, "for the church to have 200 members." When this happened, we would say that this was a noble sentiment – to put the church before themselves – but that we encouraged them to, at least for this period, release the goal of being a "noble sacrificer." When they would say things like, "but I thought I was here to serve the church," we would respond, "Yes, you are, but it's not an either/or proposition. You can serve both the church and yourself at the same time."

Commitment: a Gift You Give Yourself

I'll cover this concept of sacrifice more in depth in Chapter Seven. For now, suffice it to say that if you want to feel safe to make commitments, it is very important to release your belief in sacrifice. If you don't, you will continue to believe that commitment is something you do for someone else, that commitments are things you make to other people, and that both of you are imprisoned by them.

Speaking as a man, and also as a minister who performs my share of weddings, I am often saddened by comments I hear from groomsmen to grooms. "You better enjoy these last moments of freedom," some of them say, "before you're attached to the old ball and chain," or, "I hope you sowed your wild oats, because now it's time to settle down and forget about having fun." Comments like this reflect the common belief that the commitment we call marriage is one we do for our partners, not for ourselves. Commitment, we think, is a kind of prison which we must endure if we want the things which come with it. The reason this thought is so widespread is because our belief in sacrifice is just as widespread.

I am happy to report that my marriage is not this kind of experience. For Lura and me, our first commitment is to our relationship with God in us as our Source. Second, and as a part of knowing ourselves as spiritual beings, we are committed to our spiritual growth. Third, we are committed to being each other's true friend, to being on each other's side, and to supporting each other in being all we say we want to be in life. This means that the commitment we make (which we do daily) is one which results in *more* freedom, not less. The reason this is so is because one part of our commitment is to remove the sacrifice from our relationship.

In the marriage ceremonies at which I officiate, I include a section where I talk about love being a kind of refining fire, in which anything within us unlike our divine selves will rise to the surface. I also tell couples that if they have fights, it doesn't mean something bad, either about them or about their relationship. It simply means that the love and the commitment has resulted in enough safety for the next issue to arise. I also encourage them to practice the thought that no one needs to sacrifice in order for the marriage to work. This way, the commitment can result in more freedom, not less.

One of the more powerful ideas in *A Course In Miracles* is that God never asks any of us for sacrifice. My experience, and that of many others, has borne this out. A relationship based on sacrifice is not really based on love but on fear, and on a kind of use-use mentality.

Commitment is Freedom

Many people who are afraid of commitment say they are afraid that they will commit to the wrong thing (or person, or relationship). Then, they fear, the right thing, or person, or relationship will come along and they'll be trapped. So they entertain the thought that they just want to keep all the options open. This, they tell themselves, is freedom.

However, "keeping all the options open" is not freedom at all but prison. In my own life, and in the lives of the students with whom I've worked, I have found that fear of commitment is a cover for fear of success, fear of love, and fear of emotional healing. It is a way to keep a lid on very powerful emotions which would begin to spill out if a commitment was made. Continually sitting on the fence simply results in a part of our anatomy becoming very sore.

If you have ever thought, "What if I commit to the wrong person?" or "What if I commit to the wrong job?" or "What if I commit to the wrong dream?" you might enjoy hearing about a couple who were afraid to commit. These two first called the relationship they were in an "uncommitted committed relationship." They felt a lot of love for each other but couldn't live together. At one point they decided to see a psychic. They wanted to ask the question, "Is this the right relationship for us? Should we commit to it?" What they wanted, of course, was a clear "yes" or "no." They wanted the psychic to look into the future and, with this knowledge, tell them whether or not it was safe to make a commitment.

Instead, the psychic said, "Would you like it to be the right relationship?" She went on to give them a piece of advice I have found to be very valuable on several occasions, saying, "If you first give the decision to God, it's always safe to commit. *You can't actually commit to the 'wrong' thing.* If you first give the situation to the Holy Spirit, and if you then make the commitment, one of two things is going to happen. The situation is either going to get much better, or it is going to become intolerable. On the other hand, if you don't commit, things will probably stay about the same as they are now, except your backside will get sorer and sorer." In the case of this couple, they did commit more fully, and, as a result, came to realize it wasn't going to work.

"Asking" with Our Actions

There's a quaint old story about this principle that resources follow commitment. It comes to us from the Old West. There used to be (perhaps there still is) a kind of watering trough used in remote locations on cattle ranches. It would only fill the trough with water when a cow would step on the ramp leading up to it. In other words, the weight of the cow would open the faucet. In the story, an "old-timer" cow was showing a newcomer the ropes. The old-timer led the newcomer to the side of the watering tank and said, "This is where we drink." The rookie replied, "There's no water in this tank." The old-timer said, "No, but there will be as soon as you walk up that ramp. Your weight makes it fill with water." The newcomer replied, "Oh, sure. This is the same joke you play on all the newcomers, right? I fall for this, and you all stand there laughing at me." The old-timer said, "Okay, have it your way. But sooner or later, you are going to get very thirsty. When you do, you will find that when you put your full weight on that ramp, then there will be plenty of water for you to drink."

Jesus said, "Ask, and you will receive. Seek, and you will find. Knock, and the door will be opened." (Mt. 7:7) I notice that he did not say, "Ask, and every once in a while you will receive." Nor did he say, "Seek, and occasionally you will find." Nor did he teach, "Knock, and it's possible that the door might open." Instead, he said, "Ask, and you *will* receive." But asking isn't something we only do with our words. Some of us think our actions can all be on the side of *not* asking, and our words alone will be enough. This is not how it works. As W. N. Murray said, "The moment one definitely commits oneself, *then* Providence moves also. All sorts of things occur to help one which otherwise would never have occurred." In other words, the largest part of "asking" is making the commitment and then putting the full weight of our actions behind the commitment we have made.

Moses' Demonstration of Commitment

When I think of people who have demonstrated this, one who always comes first to mind is Moses. Like most of us who have accepted an assignment from God in us, he didn't think he was ready. Having committed a capital offense in Egypt, he also probably thought that if he went back there, he would either be jailed or killed. He had been living in a wilderness area for many years and had a wife and family there. The problem was – there was this burning bush.

If you recall the story in Exodus, Moses saw a "bush which was burning but which would not be consumed." This is not a story about a literal event. In Aramaic, a "burning bush which will not be consumed" is an idiom which means "a big problem." In this case, the problem was the *vision* which Moses had, one which lived in his heart. He believed that God had spoken to him saying, "It's time for your countrymen to be freed from slavery in Egypt, and you're the one to lead them." This was the burning bush in his heart, and the fire wouldn't go out.

If Moses was anything like the rest of us, the inner conversation he had at this point might have gone something like this:

"It's time for the Israelites to be released from captivity in Egypt."
"What does that have to do with me?"
"I want you to lead them."
"Go away."
"You're the one."
"I'm not listening."
"This is yours to do."
"I'll be killed if I go back there."
"You know you are the one to do it."
"I'm no public speaker. Send my brother, Aaron."
"Fine. Take him with you, but you are the one to lead."

So Moses finally said "yes" to God. There was then a lengthy drama with ten plagues, and then Pharaoh finally let the Israelites go. At that point, even though the Israelites left as hurriedly as they could, Pharaoh changed his mind again. He said to himself, "What have I done? I have just released most of my slave labor, and I have pyramids to build. I must get them back." So he sent his army after them.

The Israelites got to the Red Sea. They were right at water's edge, and they saw Pharaoh's army coming. They looked at Moses, the man who had led them here, and they said to him, in effect: "What? There weren't enough graves in Egypt? You had to bring us all the way out here to die?" Such a human response!

Then Moses said, "Stand still, and see the salvation of the Lord, which shall be performed for you this day." As Moses listened to God in him, he heard these words: "If you want to cross the sea, you are going to have to put your feet in the water first. Then I will help you cross the sea." Moses followed his guidance. One more time, he was told that the resources would follow as soon as he made a commitment.

As to what happened next, you can either believe Cecil B. DeMille's version or you can hear a version which is probably much closer to the truth. According to Dr. George Lamsa, the place where the Israelites crossed the Red Sea is also called the Sea of Reeds. Before the days of dredging, it was a very shallow part of the sea. The Bible story says, "And the Lord made a strong east wind (a wind from an unusual direction) to blow all night." As a result of the wind and the tide, the sea was shallow enough here for them to walk across it. The real miracle of the story (from the Israelites' point of view) could easily have been the timing. By the time the Egyptians got there the wind had shifted, and the tide was coming in. At the very same place where the Israelites had crossed, Pharaoh's army was drowned as they tried to follow.

Breaking Through Our Inner Barriers

The Israelites had been in a land where they were slaves. They wanted to go to a place "flowing with milk and honey" where they could be free. There was a barrier in the way. Isn't that always the way? No matter what we say we want, no matter how we want to change our lives for the better, once we commit to it there always seems to be a barrier, something in the way, something which, if we believe our body's eyes, looks insurmountable.

Then we hear the voice of Spirit say, "If you will stand still and ask Me, I will tell you what to do." When we hear this, it is always a relief. "That's right," we remind ourselves, "I'm not on my own here." Then when the voice of Spirit tells us how to cross the Red Sea, (move through the apparent obstacle) we are likely to again be afraid and to think that Spirit is crazy. "You want me to do what? Put my feet in the water, actually begin to move without knowing where the resources will come from?" Our human mind always wants to say, "First show me the master plan, and then I'll take a step."

This last ego wish, the one where I want to first wait to see the master plan before I take action, has never worked for me. What I notice in my life, as I ask for one thing after another that I don't know how I will have, is that commitment always comes first. Once I commit to having what I want *and begin to live my life as if I will have it*, the Voice for God always gives me at least one action step to take. I can make a treasure map. I can start a bank account. I can do whatever it takes to get information about what I want. I can write affirmations. There is always something to do. Hardly ever do I get to see the grand plan in advance. As I think of it now, I can't remember a time when I saw the whole plan before I started out. But there is always one step to take.

Then, there is almost always a barrier which presents itself, something in the way which I didn't know would be there when I began. When this happens, I stop to listen to my guidance. It tells me how to "put legs on my prayers," how to put my feet in the water, how to "act as if" this barrier isn't real but is, instead, a manifestation of my inner resistance to having this much success in my life. As I move forward, then Providence moves also, and it looks like miracles happen.

How-To's Always Follow Intention

A Course In Miracles, says that, along with resources following commitment, a twin principle is true: *How-to's follow intention.* It says that many of us have the thought that we would change, grow, become all we could be if only the right technique or teacher would show up. This, it says, is backward. The right tools, how-to's, and techniques will always show up when our intention increases to the point where we insist on it.

What would you be dreaming right now if you didn't first have to know how you would achieve it? How would you insist on changing your life if you didn't first have to wait for the right techniques to show up? What would you ask Spirit for if you didn't have to first know how it would come into being?

Whatever your dreams are, now is a good time to take them out, dust them off, and move toward having them. As W. N. Murray said, "Whatever you can do, or dream you can, begin it." As you do commit and take action, the resources will follow, and it will look like miracles are happening. You *can* manifest your dreams, one step at a time.

CHAPTER SIX

Our Power of Creation, the Male Side

There is an old story about a couple who gave birth to a son. They loved their son very much, both of them devoting themselves to his care and enjoying each new stage of his growth. Then, when he was three years old, they got pregnant again. They were both worried about how their first-born would react to his new sibling, now that the newborn would receive so much attention and love. They were even worried that the older child might hurt his baby sister, having heard stories about how difficult it is for the firstborn when he or she has to share the spotlight.

Because of this fear, the parents made sure to never leave the two children alone together. But then, one day when the father and mother were engrossed in conversation, and the baby was asleep in her room, the inevitable happened. Suddenly, they realized that the toddler was no longer in sight. They rushed into the baby's room just in time to hear her older brother say, as he looked through the bars of the crib, "Tell me about God. I'm starting to forget."

Whenever I've repeated that story to an audience, or heard it repeated by another speaker in church, there is almost an audible sigh. It always seems to resonate in everyone's body. I think the reason for this is that there is so much truth in it. As little children, we were all more aware of our oneness with God, and then we began to forget. For example, we were all extremely psychic, picking up all the energy in our household and acting it out for everyone. We knew what everyone was feeling and the essence of what they were thinking.

Then, too, there is a phenomenon which has been called "the magical child syndrome." This refers to a certain age in childhood when we believe we have magical powers, including the power to hurt or even kill people with our thoughts. To me, this syndrome is a somewhat distorted memory of how powerful our thoughts are to create our reality.

The Decision to Suppress My Power

When I was four years old, my two-year-old brother died. He was run over by a tractor while trying to follow me to a neighbor's house. As the story is told, I was supposed to be looking after him for a time while some activity happened at our house. My conscious memory is that I mostly thought of my brother as a pest. I tried to give him the slip whenever I could. I even remember having the thought that I wished he would die. Then, on this day, as he was trying to find me, he was killed as he crossed the street.

Each of us reaches a point in childhood, called "the split." This is an occasion described by Dr. Arthur Janov in his book *The Primal Scream.* It is a time when, either because of a traumatic event or because of a series of traumatic "mini-events," we shut down our real, authentic, spontaneous selves and become more unreal than real.

This was definitely the time when my split occurred. It was also a time when I made some very powerful decisions, one of which was, "Whatever you do, Phil, suppress your power. Hold yourself back. Do not allow yourself to know what you want, and definitely do not ask for it."

As an adult, many years later, I would often wonder why my life didn't work the way I thought I wanted it to work, and why I had such a difficult time knowing or asking for what I wanted. As I began to do the work of personal transformation, I came to realize why. On the one hand, I had an exaggerated, magical opinion (of which I was completely unconscious) of how powerful my thoughts were. On the other hand, I had no conscious idea that this fear was in my way.

The World According to Me

One of the tools we use in our work is a certain prayer called *The Prayer of Transformation*. This is a ten-step prayer designed to support people in releasing their inner barriers to oneness with God, as well as to instruct them in how to do this. Step Three of this prayer says, *"God is always creating my life through me, constantly giving me what I ask for through my most deeply-held decisions and emotions."* Another way of saying this is that our most deeply-held decisions and emotions are constantly creating our reality.

In Biblical symbolism, men can represent our male, thinking side, and women can represent our female, feeling side. Whenever our masculine and feminine sides unite, an offspring is always created. This means that once we make a decision about "how it is," two things happen. First, we actually begin to create our experience of life being just like that. Second, our minds become evidence gathering machines. That is to say, no matter what we decide *we* are like, or what *life* is like, or what *women* are like, or what *men* are like, we can always prove we are right by our experience.

Until we awaken to our oneness with God, this power of creation operates almost entirely on an unconscious level. Most of our "deeply-held decisions" were made so far in our distant past that the event which precipitated them is long forgotten. We create our reality according to these decisions, and then we continue to believe that we are right for thinking that the world is the way we thought it was. As it turns out, we are all living in "the world according to Garp," except that, for each of us, it is the world according to me.

I made decisions about men, women, life, God, money, work, play, and all the other categories. Then I spent my whole life, until I woke up to my power of creation, proving that I was right.

Mind, the Master Power

A wonderful old poem by James Allen called "Mind, the Master Power" describes our experience of our power of creation:

> *"Mind is the master power which molds and makes,*
> *and man is mind, and evermore he takes*
> *the tool of thought and, shaping what he wills,*
> *brings forth a thousand joys, a thousand ills.*
> *He thinks in secret, and it comes to pass.*
> *Environment is but his looking glass."*

I still remember the first time I heard the concept, some thirty years ago, that thoughts are things which produce results in the world, and that there are no such things as luck, fate, and chance. I had three reactions. The first one was that it resonated in my body as the truth. I simply knew intuitively that it was the truth, even though I didn't understand how it worked. My next reaction was to get very excited. I thought, "Could it be that easy to change my life – to have the life I want just by changing my thoughts?" Of course, it actually isn't as simple as that, which I'll be explaining in the rest of this chapter and the next one.

The final reaction I remember is that my mind began to list all the reasons why it couldn't be true. "What about the millions of Jews who died in concentration camps in World War II? What about natural disasters? What about babies? What about women and children who are abused?" These are but a few of the thoughts which raced through my head as I contemplated this idea.

Still, the concept wouldn't leave me alone. I kept thinking about it, so I decided to see whether or not it seemed true if I applied it to just *my* life and experience. As I did this, I noticed that every time I brought it back to myself, it always seemed true. Whenever I would ask myself, "Is it possible that this situation is a creation of my mind?" the answer I would hear from within was always "yes." Then, when I would look for a way in which I had something to do with what was happening, I always found a correlation.

Your Deepest Beliefs Create Your Reality

In Chapter Two, I drew the diagram I call "the screen of life" (it's on page 25). You might want to turn to it again since I will be focusing more fully on all it represents in these next two chapters. Also, because the concept outlined in this "screen" is such a major aspect of these two chapters, I'd like to review its major premises before I go any further.

I find it very helpful to see our outer world (our body, relationships, finances, etc.) as if it were the screen at a movie theater. Our mind (which includes our emotions) is the projector. The outer circle of our mind represents our conscious thoughts. This is the part of our mind of which we are aware. For most of us, this is not the part of the mind where creation occurs. Unless we are extremely conscious, creation occurs from the middle ring, the subconscious mind. This is the repository of our "most deeply-held decisions and emotions." This part of our minds is constantly projecting onto the screen of our lives the people, events, circumstances, and situations which are aligned with these so-called "core" issues. I say "so-called" core issues because the innermost circle is our *real* core. This is our God-self, our Superconscious Mind, the place where we are now and always have been one with Spirit. At this level of our being, we are one with all God's qualities – love, power, wisdom, aliveness, joy, innocence, and beauty.

During the first ten or so years of living with the concept that my mind was creating my reality, I was only aware of the *mental* part of the equation, and only dimly aware of that. As a teacher of New Thought, I talked regularly about the "subconscious mind," but I didn't have a working knowledge of mine. I also wasn't aware of the emotional component of creation.

The plus signs and the minus signs in the diagram represent what most of us would call positive and negative thoughts. An example of a positive thought would be, "I can do anything I set my mind to do." An example of a negative thought would be, "There's something wrong with me." If we have this latter thought, if it has turned into one of our "most deeply-held decisions," it got cemented into place very early in life, possibly as early as at birth, or even in the womb. As decisions like these were made, they were accompanied by very powerful emotions, such as hurt, anger, fear, and guilt. The circles around the minus signs represent these emotions, which act as a kind of "psychic glue" holding the decisions in place. If we don't open to a full experience of our emotional life, our attempts to "change our lives by changing our thoughts" will not produce much lasting effect.

In my case, as I did open to my emotional life, I began to experience change that was quite dramatic. Often, it seemed that miracles were happening.

The next stage of taking this idea deeper occurred as I became a student of *A Course In Miracles*. "*The Course*" says in many different places that not only are we creating our reality with our thoughts, but also that *everything that happens to us is our own idea.*

After using and teaching this principle for the past thirty years, it does not seem less true to me but more so. It is an incredibly exciting concept. Not only can I change my life by changing how I act, I can also alter it by changing how I think and feel. I can learn how to change my most deeply-held decisions, and I can learn how to honor, feel, and express all my emotions.

Why You Create the Experiences You Do

A big question which always arises for people as they look at the painful things they have created in their lives is "Why? Why would I create these things? Why would I want these things?" The answer to this has to do with our most powerful motivating force in life – the desire to go home. What we all want is to experience oneness with God, to release our painful belief that we could ever be separated from our Creator. In my experience, we will literally do anything and go to any lengths to reclaim our oneness with God. This is so even if we aren't conscious of this motivation.

A second factor which must be included to make sense of this principle, especially as it relates to children, is to realize that we are eternal beings. We all came to this life with an agenda of things we wanted to heal and things we wanted to receive, as well as things we wanted to give and express. No matter what our age, we are all very old souls.

A few years ago, a dear friend's daughter was dying of brain cancer at the age of about eighteen months. As the divorced parents went through this experience, they tried both traditional and non-traditional approaches to healing. They would have gone to any lengths to save their daughter's life, as would all parents. Finally, as we sat with our friend and his daughter in the hospital during her final days, Lura was holding the baby for a time and sent her the mental message: "Even now, you can be healed if you want to be." Lura said that as soon as she thought this thought, the baby opened her eyes and glared at her. Lura then heard the following thought which, she said, was as clear as a bell. "Don't mess with me. I know what I am doing." She died a few days after that.

This is but one example of people who come here for a short time and then, like this baby and like my brother, leave. Others have experiences of being neglected or abused as children. Still others live their entire lives with various handicaps or challenges. I often think that such souls wanted to grow a great deal in this life. I had this thought one day as I watched a homeless man, apparently a paranoid schizophrenic, walk down the street. One possibility is that he had previously lived a life as an "advanced" teacher. I do not believe there is any way to say which life is "better" than another.

Sometimes I hear people say, "If my entire life has been my idea, what kind of idiot or masochist would create the life I've had?" I understand this thought, since I've had it myself. I thought, "Why would I have created having two alcoholic parents?" The answer, I believe, is that I really wanted to grow a lot this lifetime. I also believe that I chose a situation which would lead me to my life's work.

We Keep Trying to Wake Up

By the time we become adults, most of us – maybe even all of us – have made major decisions which are completely out of harmony with our real selves, our divinity. Such beliefs as "There is not enough," or "Life is a struggle," or "I'm guilty for being alive," are actually intolerable to us. Because of this, we are constantly – if unconsciously – trying to bring them to the surface so that the decisions can be changed and the pain can be released.

The only way the mistaken decisions and emotional pain *can* be released is for them be brought to the surface. I've tried many other approaches, including suppressing my thoughts and feelings even more. I've even tried "transmuting" them, and being "centered" enough to not notice I have them. What I find is that, at best, these methods only *appear* to work, and then, only if I pretend I am neither creating my reality nor that the people in my life are my mirrors. However, if I can accept that neither my craziest thoughts nor my most insane feelings mean anything about my lovability, I can allow myself to become conscious to whatever is in me.

There is a wonderful treatise on the subconscious mind in *The Nature of Personal Reality*, one of the Seth books. One part of what it says is that the reason our subconscious mind is below the level of consciousness is because *we haven't wanted to know*. This has been my experience, as well. One reason we haven't wanted to know our most insane beliefs is because to remember them brings the pain to the surface. But there is an even deeper reason. *A Course In Miracles* tells us that what we really fear is what is *beneath* the pain – the memory which lives in each of us of our oneness with God.

This, then, is the other major reason why we would create situations and events which would bring our insane thoughts and emotional pain to the surface. It is as if we had (unconsciously) called "Central Casting" and said, "I have a need for someone in my life who will act thoughtless, or cruel. I have a need for a boss who will not value my contribution. I have a need for a spouse who will appear to never hear me. Would you please send one right over?" or "I need something to bring my guilt to the surface. Would you please tell me where to drive so I can get a speeding ticket?"

No matter what the situation in our lives, it is there because we want it to be there. It is there because we asked for it to be there. In the book *Illusions,* one instruction in the *"Handbook for Messiahs"* says, "Every problem comes to you with a gift in its hands." This is literally true.

Our Commitment to Wholeness

As it says in *A Course In Miracles*, "Everything which seems to happen to me I ask for, and receive as I have asked." (T. p. 448) What if we could simply accept this and, instead of resisting the things we don't like, simply begin to look for the gift instead? This is a way to greatly accelerate our transformation.

Remember the Old Testament story about Jacob wrestling with the angel and saying, "I will not let you go until you bless me?" (Gen. 32:26) This is how it is with the problems and conditions of lack in our lives. We absolutely refuse to release them until we receive the blessing, the reason we asked them to be there in the first place. Earlier, I said how futile it is to try to hate parts of ourselves enough to make them go away. It is the same for what appears to be outside us. It just doesn't work – at least, not for long. We simply find a way to have it return in another form.

In the first chapter of Genesis, the writer says, "God saw everything He had made and, behold, it was very good." (Gen. 1:31) Each of us is a cell in the body of God. One way we actually accept our oneness with God is to do likewise, to begin to say, "There is good in this, and I insist on seeing it."

The rest of the step I mentioned earlier from *The Prayer of Transformation*, says, *"There is some gift I want from every condition or creation in my life. I am now open to see and receive each gift."*

Anything We Love Will Reveal its Secrets

One of my heroes is George Washington Carver. Carver is a giant because of the size of his vision and the effect of his work. Before he came onto the scene, the farmers of the old South were becoming poorer and poorer. They only had one cash crop – cotton – and planting it year after year was depleting the soil. It was discovered that peanuts grew well in the South, and peanuts put back into the soil the nutrients which cotton removed. However, there was no market for peanuts. This is where Carver came into the picture. Through his experiments, he discovered hundreds of practical uses for peanuts, thus transforming the economy of an entire region of the country.

George Washington Carver said, "Plants are the windows through which God talks to me. The plants speak to me because I love them." He continued, "Anything you love will speak to you." I have applied this principle in a number of ways in my life. As I started to love the Bible, it began to reveal its secrets to me. As I began to love my problems, they did the same.

Once I was in a teacher training program where, for many weeks in a row, it looked like I couldn't do anything right. Each week we would have a staff meeting, and I would receive disapproval for some mistake or another I had made. I began to dread going to these meetings. One day, on the way to the meeting, I noticed how fearful I was feeling. I remembered a conversation I had had with a friend about how all our fears are actually unconscious wishes of our ego self or desires of our real self. I decided to "try on" the thought that "I love to receive disapproval." I said this phrase aloud in the car and checked in with how it felt in my body. It brought up a lot of self-judgment, but it also resonated like I was telling myself a truth! I said it again. It felt the same. By the time I got to the meeting, I knew that being on the receiving end of disapproval was definitely *my* idea. Then, after the meeting had ended, I realized that I had not received any disapproval. The next week, I did the same exercise on the way to the meeting. Same result!

I began to see that one reason I had been receiving the disapproval was that I was trying to get in touch with a deep, "core" issue. As a child, most of the attention I received was in the form of disapproval. I had decided that love and disapproval were the same thing. At my staff meetings, I had "set up" my teachers and fellow teaching assistants as my childhood family, so I could continue to resolve issues such as these. I then began to work on forgiving myself for making this decision, and I worked more deeply on forgiving my parents for (in my perception) not expressing love and approval in the ways I wanted.

To continue to use this episode from my life as an example, I found that no matter how much I told myself I hated disapproval, I couldn't eliminate it from my life. The more I hated it, the less it would "talk to me." It would only reveal the gift it had for me once I started to love it. I also found that this was a way to once again feel powerful, rather than like a victim, as I reminded myself that this situation was one I had ordered from "Central Casting."

I find this same principle at work in all the problems I have in life. All the things I tell myself I don't like are here at my invitation. They are here because I want them to be here. I am trying to awaken parts of myself to which I have been asleep. I am trying to correct mistaken decisions I have made because, even if I am completely unconscious to these decisions, they still hurt somewhere inside me.

A psychologist-teacher I knew in Hawaii, Dr. Chuck Spezzano, used to say that our experience of life reminded him of a nautical journey. Suppose, he said, we get into a boat in San Francisco and start out for Asia. While we are awake we are at the helm, and we steer the boat on a westerly course. The only problem is that we can only stay awake for a few hours each day. Whenever we are asleep, either literally or figuratively, the boat begins to head south, as if it wants to go to South America. When we awaken, we say, "What am I doing? I didn't want to go this direction. I know better than that." We then turn the boat to the west again until we fall asleep, when the scene repeats itself. In other words, we have conscious goals, and we have unconscious goals. Because of our inherent divinity, and because of our absolute insistence on being healed, our unconscious goals are always much stronger.

Where Do Our Decisions Come From?

Where do these mistaken decisions, like "Life is a struggle," and "There is something wrong with me," and "Disapproval is love," come from? They can be made as far back as our birth. They can even be made before birth, while we are in the womb. Once, in a Breath Integration Session, I relived an experience I had in the womb where I felt that my mother was trying to abort me. This experience seemed very real to me, and I felt I had made a lot of decisions based on it. Others I know have had vivid memories of their births.

Each of us "chose" our birth family based on what we wanted to accomplish this time around. For those of us who accept reincarnation as a working hypothesis, we could say that we might have made decisions a long time before this life began, and that *these* are the decisions affecting our lives today. However, in the work I have done on myself and with my students, it has almost always been enough to simply focus on this lifetime. Whatever issues we most want to heal in this lifetime are ones we recreated in our families, in our birth, and in our childhood situations.

As I mentioned in a past chapter, the first time someone vividly described the kind of birth most people my age would have experienced, I had a strong visceral reaction. I found out later that my birth had lasted for five days. After I was born, both my mother and I were exhausted, and she went directly into hemorrhoid surgery. As a result of this kind of birth, I made several decisions. "Life is a struggle," and "My presence hurts women," are two of the most obvious. Previously I had decided, "I am not wanted," and "I'm guilty for being here." These decisions affected my life in enormous ways. Before I became aware of them and worked to correct them, they ran my life. Even now, as I begin a new project or phase of my life (whenever I experience a birth of some kind), I get to say "hello" to them as they appear, although they don't have anywhere near the effect they used to have. When, or if, they do appear, it is yet another opportunity to embrace them, to love them, and to receive the gift they have for me.

Given the kind of life you have lived so far, what kinds of decisions might you have made about yourself? About men? About women? About life? In what ways have you decided, "This is how it is?" Remember, no matter how you decided life is, your mind has become an evidence gathering machine, and you can prove that the world is the way you know it to be.

As far as the effect our decisions have on our outer lives, there is another analogy I often use. It is as if we are driving with the brake on. For example, we might consciously have the thought, "I am worth a million dollars." However, we might have made an earlier decision about our worth which is very different. Then, every time we try to increase our level of income, we always find some way to sabotage ourselves.

Our First Prosperity Teachers

Many of our decisions regarding prosperity and money come from childhood, from our first teachers – our parents. Some of these lessons about money and prosperity actually had to do with money, but many of them did not. For example, many of us made the decision "There is not enough" long before we were aware of money. We made this decision in regard to our parents' love, thus giving birth to jealousy. In God's thought system, there is no such thing as competition, no need for jealousy, because there is always plenty for all. In God's thought system, there is only win/win.

Most of us, of course, did not have this experience of love when we were children. Most of our parents had shut down their hearts a long time before we came along, but we could only take it personally when it seemed we were not loved for being the person we were. In an attempt to receive what little love seemed to be available (or the approval which probably substituted for love), we competed with our siblings, or with the other parent, or with their jobs. And we felt jealous of whatever or whomever seemed to be taking them away from us.

Then, if there never did seem like enough, we may have decided, "I must not be worth loving." We also commonly decided, "I'm going to have to control and manipulate in order to have what I want in life." Or perhaps we decided, "The way to have the love I want is to act weak and helpless," (if it looked like we actually received the love we craved when we were sick).

Another huge source of our decisions was the *modeling* of our parents when we were children. We even made unconscious agreements, or "pacts," with them. One common (usually unconscious) agreement is, "I will stay little and helpless so that you can continue to have a reason to live." This agreement is often the result when one or both parents communicate to us that we are their reason for being. The fear is that if we don't need them anymore they will die, so we stop ourselves from ever succeeding. Another common agreement, especially in families where the only way "love" is expressed is through buying things and giving physical gifts, is where the children unconsciously agree to never pass their parents in success or prosperity. The fear is that if we actually become more successful than they are, we won't have parents anymore. We'll be orphans.

How We Can Change Our Deep Decisions

Decisions like these are powerful motivators and can lead to a continuous experience of self-sabotage. One effective way to change these decisions is to write affirmations. One affirmation you could write in response to either of the above unconscious decisions is, "I (name) now allow myself to be as powerful and successful as I want, even if it brings up feelings of loss." Other affirmations could be tailored to your situation if you were to work with a counselor or teacher familiar with this technique.

What did you learn about money from your parents and other influential teachers? Did you learn that "money doesn't grow on trees"? Did you learn that "the love of money is the root of all evil"? Did you hear money called "filthy lucre"? When you asked for something, did you hear statements from your parents about how "We're not made of money" or "Your father (or mother) worked very hard for this money"?

If any of us heard this last statement, we could have easily decided, "When I get to be an adult, I, too, will be working very hard for my money." Then, as adults, we may have wondered why we always seem to have to work so hard.

Many of us also had the experience that money (and/or other forms of love) was withheld from us if we were "bad" – if we disobeyed, if we didn't do as we were told, if we didn't get good enough grades in school. This is why it is so common for people to decide that "I am loved for what I do," rather than "I am loved for being who I am." It is also why so many people see money as a reward.

Of course, many of us learned powerful lessons on the role of our sex in earning and/or spending money. Because, in our society, men have historically made more money for performing the same job, women commonly decide, "I can't make as much money as I could if I were a man."

A Love-Hate Relationship with Money

One of my childhood decisions about prosperity and money came from the experience I had of receiving things instead of affection and attention. My mom would often buy me a toy whenever we went somewhere. I often received a *present* from her instead of her *presence*. As I grew older and talked with some of my uncles and aunts, their experience of me was that I was "spoiled" as a child. Mine was that, although I received a lot of toys and physical things, I never got what I really wanted, which was the experience of my parents' love. One of the teachings at our school is that we can't ever get enough of what we don't actually want, and that was my experience of material prosperity as a child.

What I decided about money and prosperity as a result of this was to have a love/hate relationship with it, a "come here, go away" relationship. I worked to change this decision of "I can't have both love and money at the same time" by writing such affirmations as "The more love I have, the more money I have, and the more money I have, the more love I have."

One of Lura's memories from childhood regarding money is that of her dad. As he was leaving for his job as a high school teacher, he would say, "Well, gotta go to work so I can buy shoes for the baby." From this, she decided several things: First, he didn't like his job and didn't want to go to work. Second, he was going to it because of her (she was the baby). Third, she was guilty for being born. Fourth, she should not have any needs or wants, and she should not ask for anything, because if she did have needs and wants someone was going to suffer.

Lura has done a lot of work on this issue, including doing affirmations like, "The more I ask for what I want, the more everyone wins," and "The more people love me, the better off they are," and "Everyone is blessed whenever I arrive," and "I always know what I want, and I always ask for it."

What did you learn from your parents about receiving money? What did you learn from them about working for money? About spending money? About saving money? About being trusted with money? About being wise with money? Then, too, from their example, what did you learn about being successful? About being powerful?

Our parents were our first and most influential teachers about prosperity. We made powerful decisions from watching them, and from their interactions with us and with each other. If these decisions are out of harmony with our divinity, we will keep recreating situations which will allow us to bring these decisions to our conscious awareness. This is the only way we can change the decisions and release the emotional pain surrounding them.

A very important aspect of this concept – that we create our own reality (or that God creates it through us according to our most deeply-held decisions and emotions) is the related concept that God in us is the one Source of everything we want. This means that ultimately we are each responsible for our own success in life. It also means that we are each free to create the life we want to have.

The Upper Limits Problem

Another closely related concept to the one which says that we create our own reality is that we each have what Gay and Kathlyn Hendricks call an "upper limit" on our tolerance for success, love, joy, and ease. In their book *Centering and the Art of Intimacy,* Gay talks about when he began to be aware of his own upper limit for happiness. He says he was embarrassed to realize just how low it was (I can relate). He began to refer to hitting this self-imposed ceiling as an ULP (upper limits problem).

You can begin to identify these upper limits problems in your life. Notice the times you sabotage yourself when things are going really well. Notice how you create a problem on the first day of a vacation. Notice, as Gay Hendricks writes, how you want to create a fight on the first day of several days off. Hendricks calls this last phenomenon "the Friday Night Fights" in the work he and Kathlyn do with couples.

In the work we do at our school, we simply support our students and ourselves in continuing to raise the bar, to keep raising our upper limits, our tolerance for success, love, money, ease, and joy. This concept is another one which declares that we are, each of us, responsible for how much we can receive of everything we want in life.

Another important aspect of how to be responsible for the love and prosperity we want to receive is learning to love and value ourselves, to practice treating ourselves the way we want other people to treat us. In the past, most of us have wanted to give ourselves very little, while, at the same time, being offended when others don't give to us or remember us at our birthday or at Christmas.

Each of us is literally so powerful that we are always receiving exactly that for which we are "asking." It's just that we haven't fully understood that "asking" also includes all our actions.

How Powerful We Really Are

My favorite Bible story about how powerful we are is one where Jesus faced Pontius Pilate unafraid. As it is recorded in John 19:10 and 11, Pilate said to Jesus, "Why don't you answer me? Don't you know that I have the power of life and death over you?" Jesus responded, "You have no power at all except that which is given to you by my Father in Heaven." Using today's language, he might have said, "Pilate, you are an extra in my movie. You have no power over me at all, except that which is given to you by the Power of Creation in me. None of this would be happening unless I wanted it to happen."

This is how it is for all of us. The people in our lives are, as far as we are concerned, extras in the movie of our life. What this means is literally staggering. It means that our bosses, our spouses, our neighbors, and everyone else treats us the way we ask them to treat us. It means that the situations in our lives are not going to change until we receive the gifts we want from them. It also means that if we want a different experience in the world, the way we will have it is to look within as the place to make changes.

Previously, I referred to the book *Getting Well Again* by O. Carl and Stephanie Simonton. In one part of the book, they suggest that each reader think of the last time we were ill (with any illness) and to list the five biggest benefits we received from being sick. As I did this, I was amazed at how much I had received from my last illness. I then took it a step further. I thought, "If this is true for a physical illness, why wouldn't it be equally true for my current experience of success and money, especially for those parts of it which I tell myself are not my idea?"

One of the exercises I did in this regard was to make a list called, "What I get out of being in debt." I was astonished at how much I received from being in debt. The biggest "benefits" were that this condition helped me to hold myself back, and it enabled me to feel constantly guilty. It turned out that being in debt had everything to do with my guilt. This meant that the way to stop creating the experience of being in debt was to practice forgiving myself. I'll discuss this more in the next chapter, but it was a huge lesson for me. I was in debt because I wanted to be in debt.

This was also at a time in my life when I was feeling quite poor, so I also wrote a list called, "What I get out of feeling poor."

I still remember that the biggest thing I got out of this experience was to continue to pretend that it wasn't my idea to be here (on the planet). I realized that if I was to be prosperous and to feel successful, I would need to release the thought that being here was some kind of "sentence" or "penance." As I practiced being grateful for being here, I found myself becoming more and more prosperous.

Affirmation Writing: an Incredibly Powerful Tool

As I mentioned earlier, one of the most basic tools you can use to support yourself in changing your "most deeply-held decisions" is affirmations. The fact that you are reading this book says that you are interested in a spiritual approach to life. This being the case, it is likely that you are familiar with affirmations as a tool. If you are, I would like to suggest that you have a brand new look at affirmations, as if, in using them in the way I will outline, they were a tool you had never heard of before.

When I first began to write affirmations, I, too, had worked with them in other ways for a number of years. They often seemed to have little effect in changing parts of my life I didn't like. I had come to think that "affirming the truth" in the face of contrary appearances was either a waste of time or something even worse – an attempt to delude myself. As a New Thought minister, I had even stopped teaching my congregations to use affirmations. Then I heard about writing affirmations fifteen times each day, five times each in the first, second, and third person. My Rebirther told me about it as I began to have my first series of sessions. I then read about it in Sondra Ray's book, *I Deserve Love*. As I began to write affirmations in this way, I started to experience powerful changes in my life.

Here, then, is the method of working with affirmations which has supported thousands of us in having more of everything we want in our lives:

1. Look for a time of day which you can regularly claim as your "spiritual growth time," and let it be at least a half-hour long. Be willing to experiment with this until you find a time which works for you. Also, be willing to feel "selfish" about this. Everyone in your life will benefit as a result of you giving yourself this time.

2. Write the affirmations by hand. The act of writing the affirmations involves more of you, and thus produces more results, than does typing them.

3. Include your first name in each affirmation you write. Also, if you were called a different first name as a child than the one you now use, write your affirmations every other day using your childhood name. This is especially important if there are unpleasant memories associated with this childhood name. It is simply not possible to disown the child in you enough to find peace of mind and have the results you want in your life.

4. Write each affirmation a total of fifteen times each day. That is, write each one:

- five times in the "first person"
  (e.g., "I, Phil, always succeed.")
- five times in the "second person"
  (e.g., "You, Phil, always succeed.")
- five times in the "third person"
  (e.g., "Phil always succeeds.")

The reason to write your affirmations in all three tenses is that we all, in our past, learned to believe things about ourselves in at least three ways:

A. The thoughts and words we said to ourselves.
   (e.g. "I can't do anything right.")
   "I, Phil, always succeed."

B. The words (and even the thoughts) which others said *to* us.
(e.g. "Can't you do anything right, Phil?")
"You, Phil, always succeed."

C. The words others said *about* us to someone else.
(e.g. That Phil! He can't do anything right.")
"Phil always succeeds."

5. Use a "response column." On each sheet of paper, draw a line vertically down the page, about 1/4 the distance from the right-hand edge. The area to the right of this line will be your response column.

6. Pause to take a breath after each affirmation you write. Before you write the response, pause and take a deep, oral breath (both in and out through your mouth). This is an ancient Yogic technique, recently rediscovered in the West, which will help you become more aware, especially of your emotions. As you become more aware of the feelings, thoughts, and body sensations which arise from writing the affirmation, write them down in your response column.

7. Do your best not to censor or edit your responses, and try to not talk yourself out of any which seem negative. This notebook is not one to share with anyone (unless you choose to share it with a counselor or teacher), so be willing to even include four-letter words and thoughts which don't seem to make sense.

Remember, the purpose of writing these responses is to become aware of the thoughts and emotions which you subconsciously hold *and which you are not aware of thinking or feeling.* It is, after all, your most deeply-held beliefs and emotions which are creating your reality, not the ones of which you are most aware. The more conscious you become, the more you can release suppressed, self-limiting beliefs and emotional pain. You will discover that the longer you work with an affirmation, the more positive your thoughts and exhilarating your feelings will be as you write it.

It will serve you highly to pay particular attention to your emotional responses. *Creation happens when thoughts and feelings are aligned.* Especially if you are one of the many of us who have been "out of touch" with how we feel, you will want to ask yourself, each time you write an affirmation and pause to take a breath, "How am I feeling right now? What is the name of the emotion?" It would also serve you to let this period of time be one in which you release the goal of "being centered" or "feeling peaceful." Spiritual success actually does mean these things, of course, but if you will give yourself a time to simply feel and think whatever you feel and think (instead of only what your parents and others taught you is acceptable), you will eventually discover a new kind of inner peace, a peace which you can only have from fully accepting and re-integrating your emotional self.

As you begin to ask yourself, "How do I feel?" let it be O.K. with you if you don't know. Simply continue to have the intention to honor your emotional nature, and move ahead. You might write, "I feel numb," as a response. For help in knowing how you feel, you can buy a copy of Louise Hay's wonderful book, *You Can Heal Your Life.* Whenever you have an illness or physical symptom, this book is an invaluable tool. It will help you become more aware of what your body is trying to tell you by manifesting this symptom.

8. Continue to write the affirmation every day until you have an inner feeling that you really *know* it to be the truth, (to "affirm" means "to make firm) or until there doesn't seem to be any movement happening. At that point, it can be helpful to release this affirmation and choose another.

By the way, when I suggest writing affirmations "every day," I really mean six days out of seven. A day off per week can be a nice "integration day," as long as it is the same day each week rather than the day when you "don't feel like doing them." Often, that day will prove to be one in which you will make the most progress if you write them anyway.

One reminder – pertaining to any kind of transformational work – is to be aware of chemicalization. This, again, means that "whenever you claim or experience more of your divinity, any thoughts or emotions in your subconscious which are unlike it will come to the surface so they can be released." In other words, do not assume that if your body feels uncomfortable, or if powerful emotions arise, or even if some condition in your life seems to get worse, that this is a "sign from God" to stop writing this affirmation. This discomfort or confusion is temporary and is simply an indication of healing in progress. Once through it, your life will be improved.

For example, I found that when I began a program of writing prosperity affirmations, what came to the surface were all the lack and poverty thoughts in my subconscious. A lot of anger also surfaced for awhile as I thought of the many years I had *mentally* worked to change my consciousness, without my outer world changing very much. Also, during this period, it seemed like my "money issues" got even louder, and that I had even less money available to me than I did before this. However, because I was aware that this was probably "chemicalization," I kept going. As a result, my experience of prosperity – both inner and outer – improved dramatically.

When I first began using affirmations in this way, I apparently wanted to experience a lot of change in a hurry. My Rebirther would give me five or six affirmations at once to write, so that I was writing seventy-five to ninety affirmations per day. At first, I had a lot of resistance to this. My hand and arm got sore, and I wanted to quit writing them. However, after a week or so of this, I began to have a different experience. It was as if the hour or so I spent writing the affirmations each day brought a breath of sanity into a mind which I increasingly saw as having mostly insane thoughts. I began to relish this "time for myself" and to make sure I gave it to myself each morning before I gave the rest of the day to serving my congregation.

Which Affirmations Do I Write?

How does one choose affirmations to write? One way, of course, is to work with a counselor who is familiar with this technique. Also, in Appendix A, I have included a list of the most powerful prosperity affirmations I've ever written. Still another way to come up with your own affirmations is to begin with your "most negative thoughts" and turn them into affirmations.

With this last technique, you can begin with such phrases as "The trouble with money is ..." and list all the sentence completions which come to you. You can do the same with love ("The trouble with love is...") ditto with being prosperous, with success, with what you most don't like about yourself, etc. Take the "top three" from the list you want to begin with, and then see if you can create an affirmation for each negative statement. Look to the list of affirmations in Appendix A as examples of how to write an affirmation.

How to Accept Your Power of Creation

Another part of opening to your power of creation is to practice actually *accepting* this power. One way to do that is to discipline yourself to do what you say you are going to do, and to not say you are going to do things you aren't going to do. If you do say you are going to do something and then you don't do it, communicate with yourself and whoever else is involved that you have decided to change your agreement. If you leave things undone which you have said you would do, you teach yourself that you are not powerful. Work to constantly empower yourself by keeping your word. Your word is one of the most valuable assets you possess.

Still another part of accepting your power is to look for all the places in your life where you feel like a victim. You might be amazed at how many there are. Then, entertain the idea that each one is somehow your idea, and that there is a gift you want from each of these situations or you would not have created it. When I began to do this, I found that the number of ways in which I felt like a victim was staggering. I also found that the more I saw each one as my idea, the more powerful I felt. I began to have thoughts like, "If I am powerful enough to create this, imagine what will happen as I clear out my unconscious intentions."

Yet another way to cultivate your power is to practice thinking about and visualizing what you want your days to look like, rather than rehearsing what you *don't* want them to look like. In a seminar I once attended, the leader said, "Don't worry about your bills. Pay them in your mind." That is, instead of visualizing all the scenarios you don't want to have happen regarding your bills, see yourself paying them even if (especially if) you don't know how you will do that.

Look Where You Want to Go

An important principle to remember is that the mind creates in the direction it is looking. If you spend your whole day picturing what you don't want, thinking about what you don't want, and rehearsing unwanted scenes, your mind will take you there. It will create in the direction it is looking. By saying this, I am not advocating "just think positive" or "don't look at your shadow." It is very important to give yourself time to heal. It is also important, however, to move on and to take charge of visualizing what you want in your life.

A powerful way to do that is to make a treasure map. A treasure map is a pictured prayer, and it is an exceptionally powerful technique which will support you in creating the life you want. The "how-to's" for this are listed in Appendix C.

The final "how-to" I will mention in support of your power of creation is to use a tool which will help you open to the unconscious parts of yourself. Although there are many good techniques for this, the one I have found to be the most powerful is called a "Breath Integration (or Rebirthing) Session." This is a two-hour time of counseling, education, and deep, oral breathing which helps people save a lot of time in seeing how to receive the gift from some "problem" area in their lives. Before I had my first Breath Integration Session, someone I knew was having a series of them. I asked him what he thought of them, and he said, "These sessions are an express train to our divinity." And so they are. You'll find a description of Breath Integration Sessions in Appendix D.

A Course In Miracles says that there is no such thing as an accident, and that "chance plays no part in God's plan." (M. p. 26) I encourage you to join me in accepting our power of creation. There is simply no way to have real inner peace without surrendering to our divinity, and this includes accepting how powerful we are.

I'd like to close this chapter – and introduce the next one – by repeating the poem, *"Mind, the Master Power,"* changing it just a bit:

"Mind **and heart** are the master powers which mold and make,
And *we* are mind **and heart**, and evermore we take
The tools of thought **and feeling**, and, shaping what we will
Bring forth a thousand joys, a thousand ills.
We think **and feel** in secret, and it comes to pass.
Environment is but our looking glass."

CHAPTER SEVEN

Our Power of Creation, the Female Side

No discussion of our power of creation would be complete if we stopped at the mental side of it. To return to Biblical symbolism, where men often stand for our mental side and women often stand for our emotional or feeling side, this would be like trying to have a baby without involving the woman. It is the union of male and female, or deep belief and emotion, which creates the offspring or result in our lives

To also return to the theme of our purpose for being here on planet Earth, we are here for essentially two reasons: The first is to heal our sense of separation from God and each other. The second is to make a contribution. For both of these reasons, it is important – in fact essential – that we take time for our own healing process, including the healing of our emotional selves. Once we have taken this time, it is important to move on, to know that we will be in the process of healing ourselves our whole lives, even as we begin to focus on contribution and on extending our love.

There is a core in us where we are beyond hurt, or fear, or guilt, or rage, or sadness. However, the only way to let this core fully come to the surface is to embrace all our emotions, including our emotional pain. Besides, when I speak of our subconscious mind creating our reality in accord with our most deeply-held emotions, some of these deepest, most suppressed emotions are the painful ones. That's why they got suppressed in the first place, although it is, of course, very possible to suppress our joy, aliveness, and love as well.

Would You Please Push My Buttons?

By the time we get to be adults, most of us are carrying around a great deal of suppressed emotional pain. When we were children, it didn't seem to do any good (or even seemed to threaten our survival) to have our feelings. The solution most of us came up with was, "Just don't have them anymore." They are, of course, still in there, still trying to come to the surface, which is the only way they can be resolved. So, in a constant attempt to bring the suppressed pain in us to the surface, we unconsciously ask people to please "push our buttons."

An old saying reminds us that "No one can make us feel mad, bad, sad, or glad." In other words, no one can force us to feel any certain way at all. Most of us, even if we agree with this saying, still use words like, "That makes me so angry," or "Don't you lay a guilt trip on me." At our school, we make a conscious point of using different language, such as "When you do that, it brings up my anger," or, "I felt guilty when you said that." We like to remind ourselves that if we feel angry, it's because the feeling of anger was already within us, and what was said or done simply activated it, helped it to come to the surface.

We *want* to activate the anger, the fear, the guilt, the sadness, the weak and helpless feelings. Why? Because even if we are completely unconscious of them, *they still hurt.* This is why we create our reality "according to our most deeply-held beliefs *and emotions.*" In other words, some aspects of our subconscious "mind" are the feelings or emotions which lie below the horizon of our awareness.

The First Step: to Realize When We're in Hell

There is an old joke which, since I am a New Thought minister, reminded me of myself (especially the "self" I was then) when I heard it: A Jewish rabbi, a Catholic priest, and a New Thought minister suddenly found themselves in Hell. This was a stunning turn of events for all of them, and they sat in silence for a long time trying to understand what had happened. Finally, the Jewish rabbi spoke. He said, "I can't believe I'm here. It must be because of all the coveting I did." After another fairly long silence, the priest spoke. "I, too, am astonished to find myself here. It must be because I had so many impure thoughts." There was another long pause, with the rabbi and the priest looking at the New Thought minister. Finally, the rabbi said, "Well, out with it. Why are you here?" The minister said, "I'm not. This isn't Hell, and I'm not hot."

The first time I heard this joke, I winced as I laughed because it reminded me so much of myself, and of how much I didn't have an actual *experience* of God, or Heaven. My solution in those days was to simply keep denying I was in Hell and affirming I was in Heaven. I thought that if I just kept saying it loudly and often enough (even as I was suppressing my emotional pain) it would come true. There was a cartoon I once saw which also seemed to be about me. In it, a man was standing at a fork in the road. He was looking at road signs, one of which said, "This way to Heaven." The sign for the other fork said, "This way to lectures about Heaven." In the cartoon, he was scratching his head, clearly not knowing which fork to take.

In my early days of being a New Thought minister, I knew how to *think* about God and Heaven. I knew how to *give Sunday talks* about them, how to *write* about them, and how to *teach* about them. I just didn't know how to have an *experience* of them, in my heart or in my body. This actually was a repeat of a childhood solution I had devised. As a child, my way of coping had always been to find a way to leave my body and enter my head. As an adult, I did the same. When I became a New Thought minister, I used my new theology as a further justification to do the same, especially when unpleasant things would "happen to me." Even though I believed, then, that my thoughts created my reality, I thought that if something "bad" happened in my life, it meant that I had done something wrong, that I was not a good "Truth student," rather than that I was just trying to heal myself.

One Kind of Poverty: Emotional Deadness

When, through my Breath Integration (Rebirthing) Sessions, I began to experience my emotional self, it was as if a whole new world was opening to me. I began to think of the word emotion as "e-motion," which I now see as being short for "energy in motion." This is what emotion is – simply energy in motion. Before I knew how to feel and be in my body, I was very poor in emotion and in energy. If the emotional range available to us all is the keyboard of a piano, my range was perhaps the middle octave (or maybe the one just below the middle).

Many people spend their entire lives in this position. Their primary goal is to avoid feeling bad. The best it gets for them is when it doesn't hurt. They never get to feel intense joy, love, or aliveness. In part, this is because they are afraid to face and feel the emotional pain inside them.

There are, of course, numerous ways to suppress our emotional life, our "energy in motion." There are drugs and alcohol, cigarettes, and food. There is work and being a workaholic. There is television, and sleep, and sex, and gambling, and shopping. There are any number of ways to "stuff our feelings."

One good time to get in touch with how you are feeling is anytime you are "stuck," whenever you don't seem to be able to move forward in life. A good question to ask yourself at such a time is, "What am I afraid to feel right now?" When you finally begin to let yourself feel it, you will find yourself moving again. Emotion really is energy in motion. Another good time is if you find yourself exhibiting any symptoms of suppressed emotional pain. A list of such symptoms is included in Appendix E.

One reason I continued on my path of transformation – once I realized that it was a path of emotional healing – is because of some reading I had done about the Russian mystic, G. I. Gurdjieff. He maintained that the shortest route to God is through our emotional center. This has been my experience, as well. An old Sunday school adage says it this way: "The only way to know God is to feel God." The place where I experience oneness with God is in my heart, when I am "in my body." There are times when I feel so much love for whoever is in my presence that it seems overwhelming. Then, my heart simply fills with gratitude to God for leading me to this path of personal transformation. This is what we all deserve – to know our oneness with God, not as an intellectual exercise but as an experience in our hearts.

Dying from a Broken Heart

The number-one cause of death in the United States is "dying from a broken heart." The worldly term we have for this is "having a heart attack." Actually, all physical pain is unexpressed emotional pain. Having a heart attack is just one way unexpressed emotional pain is acted out. People who have heart attacks are people who just simply gave up on love. They learned to shut down their hearts at an early age, and continued to try to shut it down their whole lives, dying inside a little at a time.

Before I began on the path of transformation, I was one of those people. At the age of thirty-five, I was already beginning to feel pain in my chest. As I sat at rest, I could feel my heart beating. Then, as I breathed into opening my heart (in Breath Integration Sessions), I felt like I was going to have a heart attack. Then I would start to cry. I would cry, and cry, and cry. This happened many times. It also happens quite regularly with my students.

I was amused to read a similar story in one of Jack Kornfield's books, *A Path With Heart (page 231)*. It happened while he was leading a meditation retreat in Boston. One student at the retreat was an M.D. At one point, the doctor came up to Mr. Kornfield and asked him where the nearest hospital was. He had no doubt at all that he was having a heart attack. The only advice he sought from the retreat leader was whether to drive himself or to have someone drive him. Mr. Kornfield assured him that the symptoms he described were fairly normal, ones that regularly occur as students open their hearts and get back in their bodies. This has been my experience as well. As we open to the love in our hearts, we then begin to *consciously* feel the pain which we have been *unconsciously* experiencing all along. This symptom is temporary, and it eases as we open to and embrace it.

Other Experiences of Dis-Ease

Cancer and arthritis are other diseases which are the result of suppressed emotional pain. Cancer is what happens when something has been eating away at us for a long time and we are afraid to feel the feelings associated with it. (Cancer patients are often referred to as some of the "nicest" people anyone could know.)

Arthritis is an inflammation of the joints. Once, several years ago, I saw a commercial advertising some kind of "pain killer." (Actually, there is no such thing as a pain killer.) In the ad, a kindly, old grandmother had arthritis. She was complaining because the pain kept her from doing things, including making birthday cakes for her granddaughter. Then there was some kind of jingle like, "I haven't got time for the pain," (I suggest that we can't afford to *not* take time to feel the pain) and she took the pain pill. This allowed her to be numb enough to go ahead and make the cake. The last shot was of the granddaughter saying, "I love you, grandma."

As I watched this, I thought that Grandma might just be somewhat resentful that the only way she thinks she can have the love she wants is to do for others. She cannot, however, allow herself to feel angry about this. She's too nice. So she manifests arthritis instead and takes a drug for the pain. It might be really profound for her to express her angry feelings by beating on a bed or yelling into a pillow. She might be quite surprised at how much the pain goes away.

I once attended a workshop in Hawaii led by a professor from Arizona named Dr. Roger Daldrupp. He called the anger workshop a session on "unfinished business," and he showed videos of how completely such physical symptoms as arthritis cleared up as people felt and expressed their angry feelings.

The concept that we are creating our reality according to our most deeply-held beliefs *and emotions* is true for our physical bodies. It is also true for our financial bodies, our prosperity life. The feelings we cannot feel and express are as much in our way with money, career, and prosperity as they are impediments to our physical health. The following, then, are some suggestions about specific emotions and what to do with them.

Healing Your Relationship with Anger

Anger is the first emotion I would like to address because it is the one which many of us fear the most. It is also one which keeps a lot of people stuck in failure and lack. One of the "unconscious patterns" we list at some of our workshops is: *"If we cannot feel and express our anger openly, we will act it out or express it covertly."* There is a bumper sticker which reads, "I don't get mad. I get even." Whenever I see this bumper sticker, I think to myself, "I don't know why people brag about that. *Everyone* who is unable to get mad gets even." Everyone who can't get mad has no choice but to express the anger covertly.

What I have learned in twenty-plus years of working with people is that *anger is always expressed.* However, when we were children, nearly all of us learned by experience that expressing it directly was a bad idea. Usually, our parents were also very uncomfortable with *their* anger. They had learned from their parents to suppress angry feelings, so they taught us to do the same.

When our parents were children, their parents disapproved of them when they got angry, sometimes threatening to withhold love from them at these times. This was often reinforced by an old psychological view of people. According to this theory, the core of us is animalistic, and we must all be controlled. The continuation of this thought is that if we can be enough "in control," we can be socialized and get along. "Therefore," our parents learned, "the more we can control ourselves, the better our lives work."

Into this world, we were born. Then, when we had angry feelings, our parents disapproved of us. After all, if we were angry in their presence it would begin to bring *their* own anger to the surface, anger of which they were still afraid. Our parents might have done what their parents did – threatened to take *their* love away from *us* if *we* expressed angry feelings. So we, too, learned to suppress these feelings.

Anger is Always Expressed

However, *angry feelings always get expressed in some way*. We all got very good at being covert with the anger. If we couldn't express it directly, we did so in ways which would "get back at them," especially if we could find ways which wouldn't result in us getting punished. Basically, we all got very good at "guerilla warfare." Some common ways of getting even include:

- to give someone the silent treatment
- to withhold love
- to "forget" to do what we said we were going to do (including to forget birthdays and anniversaries)
- to slow down while we do our chores
- to be constantly late
- to not receive someone's expression of love
- to not let someone win with us

However, *the most common way to get even is to fail,* especially if our parents wanted us to succeed. Sometimes parents even think the success of their children means something about their own value. Then it can be an even "better" way to get even. We can fail in school, at our jobs, and in relationships. Conversely, we can "succeed to get even" if our parents taught us that "we would never amount to anything" or words to that effect. The only problem with this is that there is no joy in succeeding at the effect of anger. We can never have enough things or money or fame to make up for the pain we feel if we believe that the most important people in our lives see us as failures.

Because these emotions run so deep, it is not at all uncommon for us to get even with our parents (and those people we have "set up" as our parents, like spouses, bosses, and the government) far into our adulthood, even into old age. Also, no matter what means we have chosen as our way (or ways) to get even, we are, of course, always only getting even with ourselves. So it is really important to learn how to appropriately feel and express angry feelings.

Yet another reason to learn how to feel and express angry feelings appropriately is that whenever we claim, express, or receive more love in any form, it brings to the surface anything within us which is unlike it. This means that if we are to claim more love, success, and prosperity, it is going to bring more and more of our emotional pain to the surface. Then, if we can't feel it, we will find a way to push away what we said we wanted in an effort to once again stuff our feelings.

Fear of Anger: a Barrier to Aliveness

My history with emotions is that I couldn't feel or express much of anything until about the age of thirty-five. As a child, I decided that it was a bad idea to express anger, sadness, and fear. What I remember hearing is that crying and being afraid were for sissies, so I learned to suppress my tears and my fears. I also was terrified of being angry. My dad was a "rage-aholic" along with being an alcoholic, so the rest of us tiptoed around the house, as if we were walking on eggshells. I became an expert at suppressing my anger and at getting even. My favorite way, I'm not proud to say, was by giving people the silent treatment. I would just sulk.

I also learned to "go into my head" whenever I was afraid instead of being in my body. By the time I was an adult, I believed I had to have a *reason* to have an emotion. So, whenever I would feel something, I would go into my head and ask myself, "Does this feeling make sense right now? Is it warranted?" Perhaps you can imagine how spontaneous and alive I was.

Because of how much suppressed anger was in me, I would begin to feel angry whenever I received love or succeeded at something. Then, I would go into my head and, because there was no "good reason" to be feeling this way, I would immediately suppress it again. This had the effect of keeping me stuck a lot in unconscious patterns. It also meant that I was pushing away a great deal of love and success.

As I shared earlier, my transformation began in Florida, when I was in a *Master Mind* prayer group. Each week I would ask God to "change me at depth." At the same time, the size of my congregation had doubled, and I was supervising the construction of a $350,000 church. Both of these things represented a lot of success and brought up a lot of anger. For example, it seemed to me that none of the workmen on the construction project would do what I wanted them to do.

It was as if I was driving with one foot on the gas pedal and the other one on the brake. On the one hand, I had all this success happening, bringing up in me all the old decisions I had made about being a failure, and the feelings of anger which went with these decisions. On the other hand, I had this inner voice saying, "Whatever you do, don't feel your feelings." So, while I was being very successful in my career as a New Thought minister, I was angry all the time. This created an enormous amount of conflict in me, and also resulted in my being depressed a lot. Now I can understand why. *I was depressed because I was "depressing" so much of what wanted to come to the surface.*

Healing the Five-Year Old in You

If you want to learn how to feel and express angry feelings, you are going to meet a frightened five-year-old (or four- or three-year-old) inside you. This child still lives in you, and you will find yourself feeling every bit as frightened to express anger *now* as you did then. This will be so even as you consciously realize that there is no rational basis for your fear. Because of this, having the support of a teacher or counselor will make it much more likely that you will actually give this experience to yourself.

After moving to Hawaii, I began to have a series of Breath Integration Sessions, and I received an assignment to have daily "temper tantrums." The idea was to devote a period each day, say three to five minutes, when I would lie on a bed, scissor my legs up and down, and scream into a pillow, as if I was a child having a tantrum. My breath coach asked me if there was any certain time of day when I felt particularly irritable. I still smoked at this time, and I said, "When I get up in the morning, I usually have to have three or four cigarettes before I can talk to anyone." He then suggested that I have a tantrum each day as soon as I got up. I was to go back to being little Phil at those times, and let him yell *now* everything he might have wanted to yell *back then*. Also, since my apartment complex had a pool, another way I could practice expressing angry feelings was to yell and have tantrums under the water.

I couldn't believe how much fear came up for me about yelling. The outside wall of the apartment I lived in was made of glass and sliding doors, which were almost always open. I was positive that the neighbors could hear every syllable I yelled (even though I was yelling into a pillow), and that the police were going to come and take me away. This experience was so fearful for me that I realized it wasn't possible for it to be a "current day" experience. And it wasn't. The five-year-old in me was still alive, still making my decisions for me, still keeping me stuck in an experience of acting out my anger instead of expressing it appropriately.

The first week I had the assignment, I think I actually did it once. On the other days, I either "forgot" or was sure I wasn't at all angry when I got out of bed. My breath coach assured me that this was normal, and that my anger hadn't actually gone anywhere. It was still there running my life. The next week I recommitted to the assignment, and did it three times. The third week I may have done it five times. It took me several weeks to actually feel any anger as I shouted into my pillow the things which the five-year-old in me might have wanted to say. ("Where are you Mom/Dad? I need you. Pay attention to me. I hate it when you're drunk," are a few examples.)

Why So Many Angry People in My Life?

As I gradually learned how to feel and appropriately express my angry feelings, I stopped having the need for people or situations to "make me angry." I stopped having the need to have so many angry people in my life, and I stopped getting even.

As I was writing this, Lura reminded me of the time when she, too, was a Breath Integration client and received an assignment to have temper tantrums. She thought her practitioner was crazy to be suggesting this. She said she had the thought, "Me? I'm not angry." But she decided to have a go at the exercise anyway. She went into a walk-in closet, sat down on the floor, and tried to think of something to yell into a pillow. After one or two half-hearted attempts, she said to herself, "I knew it. I'm not really angry."

This was at about 5 p.m. Her assignment was to release some of her angry feelings before her then husband got home, so she could be more loving to him when he arrived. After her husband entered the house, he sat down on the couch to read the newspaper. After finishing a section, he threw it on the floor. Lura said she started to yell at him about how thoughtless he was to do this. Then she continued to tell him in a loud voice about everything else he had done wrong in the fifteen years they had been together. When she had calmed down, she said to herself, "Well! Maybe I am angry, after all," and began to get more serious about doing her temper tantrum assignment.

As I said earlier, what I noticed about this idea of doing a temper tantrum each day was that even if I was angry the rest of the day, I would hardly *ever* be angry when it came time for my anger practice. My ego identity was so attached to keeping the anger and blame in place that I resisted and resisted the thought that I was angry. I did keep going with it though, and I noticed that my outer life kept improving even when I couldn't actually feel the anger as I shouted and kicked. The more I took responsibility for the emotional pain in me (instead of insisting that it was other people who had the problems and that they were no reflection of me) the better things seemed to get.

I still remember a time, a few years before I learned how to feel and express my anger, when I was living in Lee's Summit, Missouri, and attending Unity's ministerial school. For a time, I had next-door neighbors who were "at each other" all the time, yelling loudly at they argued. I actually had the self-righteous thought, "I'm sure glad I'm not like those people."

Of course, I was exactly like that. That is, these people were in my life because I wanted someone to show me this aspect of myself. They were the mirrors I had asked "Central Casting" to send. Even though I was completely unconscious of my anger, even though I did my best to keep it buried, this suppressed anger was still keeping me from having the life I wanted.

How do you know if you are angry and just don't know it? We at our school have devised a list of "symptoms of suppressed anger," which is included in Appendix E. You might want to take time now to look over this list. Also, if you want a more complete description of how to feel and express angry feelings appropriately, you'll find instructions in Appendix B.

Feeling (and Healing) Your Sadness and Fear

The same principle which applies to anger also applies to the other kinds of emotional pain which many of us carry. For example, if we have a lot of suppressed sadness inside ourselves and can't feel it or cry, we will create experiences of loss, sometimes over and over, so we can bring the sadness to the surface. We don't do this because we are stupid or masochists. We do it because we are absolutely committed to healing our sense of separation from God in us.

Often, of course, our emotions overlap. In my case, at the end of my "anger release" practice times I would often begin to cry. Gradually, it even got to be alright with me to cry when other people were present, sometimes even in public places. As I did, I had fewer and fewer experiences of loss in my life.

The same is true for fear. If we have a lot of suppressed fear, we will continually create situations which look like they scare us. In addition, our friends might very well call us "control freaks." The only reason some of us seem to want to control everyone and everything is because of suppressed fear. *A Course In Miracles* tells us that when we're in our ego mind, the ultimate goal in life becomes control instead of happiness.

The way I learned to "express" fear was to simply let my body shake with it. I found that there was an enormous amount of suppressed fear in my body. It felt good to let go of enough control to just physically shake. The more I did, the less I had frightening situations in my life. Also, the more OK it became to simply feel the fear in my body – without believing that it was either current-day or real – the less it stopped me from doing what I wanted to do.

This has everything to do with prosperity, of course. The less our fears stop us, the more likely we are to take risks, to express our good ideas, and to learn new skills. The less we believe that our fears are real, the easier it is to receive love in all forms, including money.

Releasing the Guilt You Carry

Another emotion which, if suppressed, has an enormous effect on our prosperity and success in life is guilt. Guilt is the one emotion everyone hates to feel. It is also the one with which most of us are the most familiar.

In my childhood, as I learned that I was supposed to be a "big boy," it seemed to mean that I wasn't supposed to cry or be afraid. Also, since the game we all played in my childhood family was, "Don't make Dad angry," I had already decided that it was not a good idea to get angry, or really to demonstrate any emotions at all. This pretty much left me with guilt. I grew up feeling guilty about everything. Even though I felt guilty all the time, it was such a normal experience for me that I was unconscious to it.

As I participated in my six-month program of personal transformation many years ago, one of my teachers used to say, nearly every time he walked past me, "You're not guilty, Phil." For the first few months of that program, I wondered why he did that. Then, as it became easier to feel and express my emotions, I started to realize that guilt literally oozed from every pore of my body. I looked guilty. I acted guilty. And finally, I knew what it felt like to *feel* guilty.

If we feel guilty, and if we are doing our best to suppress it, we will unconsciously look for ways to bring it to the surface. We will find a way to not keep our agreements and not even know why. We'll find ways to be out of integrity. We'll be in debt for what seems like forever, and it will seem like we can't stay debt free for very long, no matter what actions we take. Therefore, the more we can feel the guilt we carry in our bodies, take a breath into it, and remind ourselves of the spiritual truth that we can't possibly *be* guilty, the easier it is to release the need to be in debt.

During our school's first-year course, we encourage our students to get into integrity in all areas of their lives. Often, they think we are trying to get them to be "good people," that this is why we encourage them to clean things up. But that isn't it at all. What we know is that when we are out of integrity, when we don't keep the agreements we have made (including unconscious agreements as paying our taxes), we are practicing being guilty. We also know that the more we believe we are guilty, the more we create struggle in our lives. We sabotage ourselves, and we have a hard time being prosperous. Why? Because our most deeply-held beliefs are constantly creating our experiences in life.

Earlier I mentioned that I did an exercise called, "What I get out of being in debt." I found out that one of the biggest payoffs I received was to constantly have the experience that, "I am guilty just for being alive. I'm guilty just for showing up on the planet." The more I let myself feel that, breathe into it, and remind myself of the spiritual truth (which is, "Everyone, including me, is better off because I'm here"), the easier it became to get out of debt.

Those of us who believe we are guilty unconsciously demand to be punished. Many of us, in fact, have found ourselves catching a glimpse of the thought, "If only something bad would happen to me, I would feel better. If I could just be punished, I could finally let go of this feeling of guilt." It is important to know that this strategy doesn't work. It might seem to momentarily alleviate the guilt feelings, but it is truly a temporary "fix." The only thing which actually works is forgiveness – of ourselves and others.

When we believe our guilt is real, we unconsciously try to create struggle in our lives. We find ways to sabotage our successes. We insist on sacrificing. We have a very low ceiling on how well our lives can work, how much success, ease, joy, love, and prosperity we can tolerate. This means that it is incredibly important to learn how to feel the guilt in our bodies, to keep releasing it, and to keep reminding ourselves that we are inherently innocent.

Learning How to Feel: Becoming More Alive

Hopefully, you are by now thinking, "Hmm. Learning how to feel and express my feelings would be a very good idea." If so, you might well ask yourself, "How do I learn to be a feeling person if I have lived a lifetime (so far) dedicated to living in my head? How do I open to my emotional side?" There are certainly things you can do. You can write affirmations about how safe and rewarding it is to feel and express your feelings. (You will find a list in Appendix E.) You can practice recognizing the symptoms of suppressed emotions. (Again, these are summarized in Appendix E.) Another way to do this is to have a copy of Louise Hay's book *You Can Heal Your Life* on hand. It lists diseases and bodily conditions and their possible emotional and mental causes. (I have found this book to be amazingly accurate.)

You can practice having the kind of "temper tantrums" I mentioned earlier. Also, you can let yourself receive the support of a counselor, rebirther, or breath coach. But the most important thing you can do is to turn up your intention, to really *want* to feel and express your feelings. This will always result in the right methods, teachers, and "how-to's" showing up.

Forgiveness from the Heart

Most of all, we can all practice forgiveness. This has everything to do with both our ability to feel and express our emotions and with our outer results in life. The more deeply we can forgive ourselves and everyone in our past who we thought harmed us, the more prosperous we will be.

The way we teach forgiveness in our school is that it has at least three parts. The first step is letting the child in us have a time to express his or her feelings (sometimes we call this becoming conscious of the blame and attack in us). The next step is taking back our projections, and the third step is letting our lives reflect that we are not damaged.

To illustrate this forgiveness process, I will share with you a forgiveness experience I had in regard to a belief I had that I was not wanted. In a Breath Integration Session, I had the experience of being in my mother's womb. It seemed to me that my mom was having a thought something like, "Oh no. Not another child." (I was the sixth. The next older child to me was four years older, and my mom was nearly forty.) Both my parents could easily have had the thought, "Five children is enough. We don't want anymore." If they did have this thought (I could certainly see myself having it in their place), it wasn't personal to me. But I took it personally, and I thought it meant something about me. I thought it meant that there was something wrong with me.

The first step I took in my forgiveness process about this was to let little Phil have his feelings about this, and to express them as loudly as he wanted to (into a pillow, not at my physical parents). I was furious. I felt incredibly hurt. I had insane thoughts like, "All the pain I've suffered in my life was your fault." (*A Course In Miracles* would call this activity of blaming and feeling like a victim "projection.") I had temper tantrums. I cried and cried as I felt the hurt in me.

After I let the child in me say *now* what I hadn't allowed him to say when I was little, I began to work on "taking back my projections." As I was pondering how to do this, I had another Breath Integration Session in which I had the realization that I wasn't even sure I *wanted* to be born. I might have even welcomed an abortion. I believe I had the insane thought that it wasn't my idea to be here on planet Earth. From this, I realized that whatever thoughts my parents had about not wanting me were a reflection of my own thoughts. They were just showing me a part of myself. At this point, I began to work on forgiving myself for thinking that being on Earth was a bad thing. I also wrote affirmations about forgiving my parents, such as, "I forgive you, Mom and Dad for acting like you didn't want me."

Skipping Steps Doesn't Work

What has been important in our work – both in our own lives and in the lives of our students – is not to skip that first step. It can seem like a difficult or distasteful one, especially if we have a well-rehearsed "nice person" act in place. Actually, as we learn to feel and express all our feelings, it brings with it such an incredible sense of aliveness that we wonder why we were so afraid of it.

However, because we have so many cultural messages about how expressing feelings is a bad idea, some of us try to go directly to this second stage – taking back the projections – without taking time to heal our inner child and adolescent. This never works as well to bring us the results we want in our lives.

As important as it is to let ourselves become conscious of all our feelings (as well as our insane thoughts about who hurt us), it is equally important to reach the stage of "taking back our projections." Eventually, we reach a time when we realize, "The child and the teenager in me have had their say. It's time to remember that I've never been a victim. Everything, even this, was my idea." I first had the thought, "I don't think I want to be here," and then later *they* had the thought, "We don't think we want him to be here." They were just reflecting my mind back to me, which is always how it is. As we say at our school, paraphrasing *A Course In Miracles*, "There is nothing out there but aspects of ourselves being reflected back to us."

The third aspect of forgiveness is letting our lives demonstrate that we are not hurt. *A Course In Miracles* says that this is how we know whether or not forgiveness is complete. If it still looks like our life is damaged in some way, there is more forgiveness work needed.

What I did in this example was to keep including myself in current-day situations. I noticed that I had been regularly looking for evidence of how others were excluding me. It felt "normal" for me to perceive myself as being unwanted and to then feel hurt. In the past, I would stop right there. I would perceive myself as a victim, and I would judge others for their thoughtlessness.

Now, I realize that I always have a choice. I can perceive myself as being left out, or I can include myself by taking some action to join the group. Each time I join or include myself, I am demonstrating that my life was not damaged by this previously perceived hurt. It's a lot more fun, and it makes my life a much richer experience, both inwardly and outwardly.

Forgiveness: the Ultimate Prosperity How-To

Forgiving ourselves and others is the ultimate prosperity exercise. The more we forgive, the more we can accept our innocence. The more we accept our innocence, the freer we feel to give ourselves the life we deserve.

Whenever I talk about emotions to people who believe they need to be in control of them, they often say things like, "If I start crying, I'll never stop," or "If I 'give in' to my anger, there will be no bottom to it." These ego defenses are simply not true, with one exception to note. The exception is that if we are deeply angry and refuse to feel it, and if we insist on crying instead of getting angry, it can seem like there really is no end to the sadness. The same is true if anger is easy, and sadness (or fear, or guilt) is not. A counselor or teacher who has worked on his or her emotions can help you with this.

The larger fear that is hidden in the above thoughts, though, is one repeatedly voiced in *A Course In Miracles*. It says that we think we are afraid of facing our shadow. We think we fear seeing the "ugliness" in our minds and hearts, but what we are really afraid to face is our love of and oneness with God. This has been my experience, as well. The larger fear we all have is opening to the love in us, the power of creation we have, the aliveness we find through opening to our emotions, and the guidance which is always available. In short, our biggest fear really is embracing our magnificence.

Letting ourselves have our emotions is a huge key to experiencing the richness, the abundance within us. The more we feel and express the abundance within us, the more abundant our outer life becomes. Most of the goals we have, if we look deeply enough, eventually boil down to a desire to be happy and at peace. In other words, they have to do with our emotional life.

Making Friends with Your Emotions

There are several how-to's available to you if you want to open more fully to your emotions. There are affirmations to write about you and your emotions, especially in regard to the one or ones about which you have the most judgments. There are daily temper tantrums you can practice. Then, too, there is cultivating a network of friends who also want to honor *their* emotions (instead of each of you trying to get the other to "stop crying," or "don't be angry," or "there's nothing to be afraid about"). My friends and I say things to each other like, "It feels so good in my body when you let yourself express what you are feeling."

Then there is using your breath as a tool. One thing you can do is to have a series of Breath Integration Sessions or Rebirthing Sessions. There is a description of Breath Integration Sessions in Appendix D. Rebirthing uses a similar breath and, generally, has similar goals, depending on the background, training, and level of emotional healing of your Rebirther.

However, even if you never have one of these sessions, there is a way in which you can always use your breath to support you in developing your emotional life. That way is to pay attention to how you breathe. A way of breathing which will support you in opening to your emotions is to breathe orally, both in and out through your mouth, especially when you notice yourself feeling afraid and holding your breath. At those times, you can simply take a deep breath through your mouth and into your belly. Then, simply exhale without either holding on or forcing the air out of your lungs.

When we were children, we learned how to suppress our feelings, and then we practiced this a lot. The physiological way we did this was to hold our breath. We learned to be so masterful at holding our breath that we could suppress whatever we were feeling. We can now learn to be just as masterful at taking a full, oral breath when we feel frightened, sad, angry, or guilty, as well as when we feel sexual, loving, or enthused.

You really are creating your own reality according to your most deeply-held beliefs *and emotions*. The more you honor your emotional life, the more your creations will be conscious ones. As you embrace your emotions, you will find yourself experiencing the wealth of God which lives in you, and your outer world will reflect it.

CHAPTER EIGHT

Living Your Vision

In the past, many of us thought it was necessary to choose between our spirituality and our outer success. We thought we had to make a choice between the health of our soul and the well being of our pocketbook. We thought we had to decide between who we wanted to *be* and what we want to *have*. It turns out that it is not necessary to choose at all.

Dr. Emmett Fox, a New Thought writer familiar to many for his book, *The Sermon On The Mount*, also wrote a small booklet called *Your Heart's Desire*. In this booklet, which is one of my favorites, he outlines a concept which he calls the "divine plan" for our lives. In discussing this concept, he is quick to point out that he is not referring to some being "out there" named God who wants some of us to move over here and others to move over there. He is referring to the God within each of us whispering to us what is possible for our lives and how to actualize it. He says that this divine plan for each of us includes "health, wealth, happiness, and perfect self-expression." I completely agree with this list, and would add to it "loving, empowering relationships."

In his pamphlet, Dr. Fox says that this is a *uni*-verse, a place or realm where everything fits together as part of one large whole, a place where everyone has a right place, including you and me. He notes that in this universe there isn't any need for competition. By example, he says that if two-hundred of us were applying for a certain job, it couldn't possibly be the right place for all two-hundred of us. This job could only be the right place for one of us. All the rest of us have a right place somewhere else.

This concept, as I have lived it in my life and taught it to others, means that there is a way to *surrender into* our prosperity rather than to fight or compete for it. The way we do this is to realize that we are spiritual beings, living in a spiritual universe, governed by spiritual laws. Our spirituality, rather than being the *least* real part of us is actually the *most* real. We are first of all spiritual beings. Next we are mental and emotional beings, and finally we are physical beings. Our bodies are simply the outermost parts of us.

Jesus said, "In the world you have tribulation, but be of good cheer. I have overcome the world." (Jn. 16:33) He also said, "The works that I do, and even greater works than I do will you do, because I go to the Father." (Jn. 14:12) When Jesus said for us to be of good cheer because he had overcome the world, he wasn't talking about something he could do that we could not do. He was showing us the way. When he said, "I am the way, the truth, and the life," (Jn. 14:6) it was an Aramaic figure of speech. It meant, "The way to know God as I know God is to do as I do. Then *you* can do miraculous things just as *I* do miraculous things."

There has only ever been one way to oneness with God, and that is the way of personal transformation. In the early days following Jesus' resurrection and ascension, his disciples did not call themselves Christians. They called themselves "followers of the way." The word "Tao" also means "way" or "path." Some Buddhists also call themselves "followers of the way." No matter what the name of the religion, "the way" to oneness with God is the path of deep inner change.

Life is Meant to Be a Feast

Jesus encouraged us to "be in the world, but not of the world." This was the kind of life he led while he was here physically. He was very much "in the world." His first "miracle" was turning water into wine at a wedding ceremony. Imagine, the person who is often depicted as sad and somber choosing, as the first public demonstration of his ministry, the prolonging of a party!

Actually, this story is an allegory, a teaching story for each of us. In those days, people often used the drinking of wine as a symbol of being filled with God because there is a noticeable effect from ingesting it. You might recall that when the disciples were in the upper room at Pentecost, people thought they were drunk, at nine in the morning, because they were filled with the Holy Spirit.

In the story of the wedding at Cana, Jesus represents what he always does – a conscious experience of oneness with God. It is teaching us how our lives can change from plain to extraordinary when the Christ shows up in them, when we know our oneness with God. Then, instead of living lives which are drab and hum-drum, our lives are filled with Spirit. We find ourselves so filled with joy, our lives so filled with passion, that we sometimes feel giddy with it.

We Can Have Both – God and Prosperity

How different this experience is from the belief that we have to choose either fulfillment or prosperity, either spirituality or money. Many of us have believed that we had to live our lives in boxes or compartments. We thought we had to be one person at work and another person at home or in church. I have even overheard comments in the marketplace like, "Love might be a fine sentiment for old ladies and children, but business is business."

People who think like this are usually afraid of God, believing that God's will for them is completely different from their will for themselves. But the word which we translate as "will" actually means "desire." Spirit's desire for is the same as our desire for *our* children – that we are happy, and at peace, that we are successful, and that we get along with our brothers and sisters. God's will, or desire, is the same for all of us, just as our desire is that *all* of our children be happy.

According to *A Course In Miracles*, the only actual will we have is God's will. Our egos might have wishes and fantasies, but the *will* of our real self is always aligned with the desires which Spirit has for us. This means that the more we surrender to our true and real selves, the better everything gets. Our lives become more and more like a party, or, as Jesus describes them in another place, a banquet.

Before I had my first conscious experience of oneness with God and asked for God's will to be done, my life did not feel like a party. My marriage was painful, and I hated my job. As I surrendered for a moment, as I completely let go for the first time in my life, I was momentarily connected to God consciousness. Then, as I said earlier, I heard a Voice say, "You are going to be a minister." This is not a gift given to a certain few. Everyone has a calling. Each of us is called from within ourselves to make a contribution to the whole. As we surrender to this call, our lives get better and better. They also get more and more authentic.

Part of surrendering to this call is having a willingness to release our attachment to suffering. *A Course In Miracles* says that we all have an attraction to guilt and suffering. Gurdjieff agrees, saying it is the thing to which we are the most addicted. After working closely with hundreds of students through the years, I can report that this is my experience, as well. One of the necessities for surrendering to God's will and our real selves seems to be accepting that life is *supposed* to be this good.

Releasing Our Addiction to Pain

There is another teaching story from Jesus' life which speaks to this. It is the story of when He turned over the tables in the temple and withered the fig tree. These events happened during what is often called Holy Week. Just after riding triumphantly into Jerusalem, Jesus went into the temple and turned over the tables of the money changers. Then he cursed a fig tree which immediately died.

I like to write about the metaphysical meaning– the inner meaning– of this story, because it is one which has caused so much confusion among Jesus' followers. What on Earth was the representation of Divine Love doing throwing tables around and killing fig trees? The answer is that this is a teaching story, a story about how we can release our attachment to suffering.

The story began with Jesus entering the temple in Jerusalem. He looked around for awhile, saw what was going on, and then left. It was evening, so he and his disciples went to the nearby town of Bethany to spend the night. In the morning, as they were walking back to Jerusalem, Jesus saw a fig tree. As the story is written in Mark 11, Jesus said to himself, "Hmm. I'm hungry for a fig. I think I'll pick one from the tree over there." However, it wasn't fig season, so there were no ripe figs on the tree. He then said to the fig tree, in a manner of speaking typical in the Mideast, "No more will anyone eat of your fruit," and, the story says, the disciples heard him say this.

They continued walking until they came to the temple in Jerusalem. Because it was Passover time, there were people at the temple from all over the known world. Jews from many other countries had gathered there to experience Passover together. One of the biggest rites of the season was to prepare and present a sacrifice, a burnt offering. The way the priests and local temple officials had it set up was that the only acceptable way to do this was to first exchange one's foreign currency for local money, and to then buy doves, the only acceptable offering.

Over the years, this had evolved into a highly profitable business for these officials. In today's lingo, we could say that it had become a huge scam. The religious pilgrims were first charged an exorbitant rate of exchange as they traded their foreign currency for local money. Then they were charged an outrageous price for the doves, which they had no choice but to buy if they were to fulfill the reason for their pilgrimage. Into this setting walked Jesus. He turned over the tables of the money changers and drove those who were selling doves out of the temple. He said to them, "It is written, 'My house shall be called an international house of prayer,' but you have made it into a den of thieves." (Mk. 11:17)

Jesus and his disciples then walked back to Bethany. As they did, they passed the fig tree Jesus had cursed. Peter said, "Look master, the fig tree has dried up from its roots." Jesus then said something which sounds remarkable and completely out of context. He said, "Have faith in God. If you say to this mountain, 'Be removed and cast into the sea,' and do not doubt in your heart, it shall be so. And nothing shall be impossible to you." What a story! What does all this mean?

Eliminating Suffering at its Roots

To explain this as a teaching story, I will start with the metaphysical meanings of some of its aspects. Jesus, remember, represents something in each of us. He represents *a conscious experience of oneness with God*. In this story, we could also say that he represents the light of spiritual truth. The temple represents that place within us where a worship service is constantly happening. It represents that place in us where we worship what we think is the cause of our happiness (whatever and whoever have become gods to us). So at the beginning of the story, we have a moment of conscious experience of oneness with God, and that moment sheds a bit of light on our inner temple. (Jesus first visited the temple and saw what was happening.)

Next we have the village of Bethany. I looked up the word "Bethany" in Charles Fillmore's Metaphysical Bible Dictionary. (Charles Fillmore, along with his wife Myrtle, founded the Unity Movement. One of his great contributions is the Metaphysical Bible Dictionary.) According to Fillmore, the word Bethany means, in Hebrew, "house of figs." Bethany got its name because it was surrounded by groves of fig trees. These trees, says Fillmore, have two distinct characteristics. The first is that, as the figs ripen, they form a gummy substance which constantly drops from them much as tears drop from the eyes of one who is crying. The second characteristic is the wind. It blows most of the time in that area and makes a noise which resembles moaning or sighing as it moves through the fig groves. Because of this, says Fillmore, the village of Bethany represents a state of suffering or affliction in us.

Whenever we are in a state of suffering, affliction, or distress, we have, metaphysically, gone to Bethany. Most of us have been to Bethany a lot. We know about suffering. We know about feeling bad. We know about depression and despair. At our school, we often tell our students, "God doesn't want to take anything away from us – except our suffering."

Jesus and the disciples went to Bethany, and they spent the night there. This represents bringing the light of truth, or conscious awareness of oneness with God, to our state of suffering. In the morning (as the light begins to dawn on us that we are suffering and don't have to be), Jesus and his disciples were walking back to Jerusalem and the temple. They passed the fig tree, and Jesus said, "No more will anyone eat of your fruit." That is to say, "I represent the end of suffering. The way you will end the suffering in your lives is to follow me."

Next, they went to the temple, where Jesus turned over the tables of the moneychangers, and drove out those who sold doves. What this means is that, as we accept our divinity and put our relationship with God first in our lives, we discover that everything outside us that we worshipped as the cause of our happiness has, in fact, been shortchanging us.

Turning Over the Tables Inside Us

There are several meanings to turning over the tables (in our inner temple). One meaning I can relate to is that before I began to transform my life, I had everything backward. I first decided what I wanted to *have*. Then I let what I wanted to have dictate what I would *do*. And I let what I did dictate who and what I would *be*. This whole way of living – believing that something outside myself would make me happy – was definitely short-changing me. It always seemed to promise so much, and it always delivered so little. The only way which actually produced happiness was to reverse this order, to "turn over the tables" in my life.

Whenever we make a god out of anyone or anything outside us, it means we believe that they or it are the source of our love, happiness, wealth, or peace. This never produces the results we want.

Another way we can be worshipping something which short-changes us is when, from an ego point of view, we try to build ourselves up by tearing others down. This never works either, but we do it constantly until we realize our oneness with God and all the people in our lives. Still another "false god" which short-changes us is when we worship the concept of sacrifice itself.

As we all know, the concept of sacrifice has long been taught as a virtue. Most of us have, in fact, been taught that the way to be more spiritual is to be more sacrificial. Actually, as we look at the history of religion in the world, one way of seeing that history is that it is the evolution of the concept of sacrifice.

It's Time to Stop Sacrificing

Most, if not all, ancient religions practiced human sacrifice. It was thought that this is what we needed to do to appease angry gods. *A Course In Miracles* would tell us that our belief that God (or the gods) wanted sacrifice was a matter of projection. We, in believing that we could separate ourselves from God, thought we had made the ultimate sacrifice. Because of this, we decided that God wanted us to sacrifice. The end of this practice, at least in the Judeo-Christian tradition, was when Abraham "heard" God tell him to sacrifice his only son, Isaac.

How did Abraham hear God tell him to do this? The same way *we* hear God, of course – as an inner thought. Abraham thought he heard God tell him to kill his son. This would have been a normal thing to hear in those days. Would the God we know ask us to sacrifice a child? Of course not. Neither would God have told Abraham to kill his son. But Abraham "heard" this because it was something commonly practiced by deeply religious people in his day. As he was preparing to kill Isaac, the light dawned in his mind. He saw a goat caught in a bush, and this gave rise to another thought: "God doesn't want me to sacrifice my son. This goat would be an acceptable substitute."

Of course, the God we know would no more ask us to kill a goat to appease Him/Her/It than would Spirit ask us to kill a child. But in the Old Testament, animal sacrifices were thought to be either acceptable or unacceptable to God because of their odor. When Jesus began his ministry, he was born into this consciousness of sacrifice. When he decided that his ministry would include his death and resurrection, people simply couldn't see it as anything other than that – a sacrifice. So we, as a race of people who felt separated from God, manufactured this concept that the only way we would get to Heaven was to accept that Jesus died for our sins. After all, we thought, *someone* has to sacrifice *something*. We had no idea how much we were projecting our human qualities onto God. Our belief that God needs, wants, or can't do without sacrifices is simply our spiritual immaturity.

To release sacrifice from our lives requires basically one thing – that we include ourselves as one of the receivers of the gift we give. What if Jesus was also receiving something from his incredible demonstration of mastery over death? What if his entire life – not just his death – was lived not only for us *but for himself also*? It would completely support us to release our belief that sacrifice equals spirituality.

Jesus' reference to being the "lamb of God" did not mean that he saw himself as being led to the slaughter. It was his way of describing himself as completely trusting, willing to follow wherever his inner Shepherd asked him to go.

TheW heal$ad

When I was a student in my six-month program of personal transformation, I learned about something called "The Wheel of Sacrifice," which we now teach to our students so they can see if they are on this endless wheel. Imagine a wheel, or circle, with four points on it. The top point is guilt, the emotion which is so familiar to most of us, the one we try so hard to suppress. As I mentioned in the last chapter, when we feel guilty, one of the ways we try to alleviate the feeling is to sacrifice. So, moving around the circle clockwise, sacrifice is the next point.

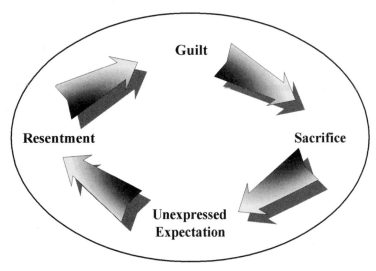

The Wheel of Sacrifice

To sacrifice means to do something for someone else in which we don't include ourselves as one of the receivers of our own gift. It means to give to others in the belief that we are separate from them. It means to do something we don't actually want to do, but which we are afraid *not* to do. We do this because we believe we are the other person's source and that he or she is our source.

We sacrifice when it is "our turn" in co-dependant relationships, so that when it is later our partner's turn to sacrifice, he or she will return the favor. This is what the world would call a "normal relationship." It is what *A Course In Miracles* would call a "special love relationship" (as compared to a holy relationship). The unexpressed expectation with sacrifice is that if we do things "for others" when they need us, others will do the same for us when it is our turn to need them.

Unexpressed expectation is the next point on the circle. It is unexpressed because we never actually say, up front, what we want from those for whom we sacrifice. It is just understood. And, because it is unexpressed, it always leads to disappointment. If you have ever found yourself saying (as I have), "After all I've done for you ..." you can be sure that you were sacrificing as much as I was when I heard those words come out of my mouth.

Unexpressed expectation leads immediately to resentment. We can all, no doubt, hear the resentment in the above statement. This is the next point on the wheel. And, because resentment is so completely out of integrity with our divinity, the next emotion we feel is guilt. At this point, we begin another ride around the wheel.

For centuries, we have believed that love and sacrifice are the same things. The mistake we have all made is *not including ourselves as one of the receivers* of our gift. *A Course In Miracles* tells us that everything we give is given to ourselves.

God Never Asks Us to Sacrifice

It is always possible to include ourselves as one of the receivers as we give. God doesn't want any kind of sacrifice from us and never asks us to sacrifice our own best interests. The only thing Spirit asks us to do is to extend love, just as *It* extends love. This is what makes it possible to release the fear of God, so that we can actually *want* to have a personal relationship with Spirit.

We are not here in this life to suffer, to be martyrs, or to sacrifice. *We are here to heal our sense of separation from God and from each other, and we are here to express ourselves, to make a contribution to the whole, to create something.* This is our two-fold purpose for being here on planet Earth.

The first part of that purpose is, of course, something we all have in common, and we are doing this whether we are conscious of it or not. It is also one way in which we are all the same, just like the cells in our bodies have many ways in which *they* are all the same. No matter if they are muscle, nerve, bone, or blood cells, they are all made of the same basic stuff. So are we.

Like the cells in our bodies, though, there is also a way in which we are all unique. Each of us is also a cell – in the body of Christ or the body of God. Each of us comes to this life with a unique set of talents, interests, and abilities. There are things you can do which I cannot, and vice versa. There are things which you can do with ease and grace, things which would be an enormous struggle for me. There are things in which I am interested enough to become accomplished. These same things would be either boring or not worth it for you to learn.

Each of us brings to the table something unique, something to contribute to the whole. I believe it was Marshall McLuhan who said, "There are no passengers on spaceship Earth. Everyone is crew." Everyone's part is essential to the success of the whole.

How to Discover Your Mission in Life

How do you find the part that you came here to play? What is your purpose for being here? What is that "perfect self-expression" to which Emmett Fox refers in his pamphlet? According to Fox, the answer is "divinely simple." It means asking yourself:

- What do I love to do?
- What do I feel passionate about doing?
- If I could express myself any way I wanted to, how would it be?
- What enlivens me and brings me joy as I do it?
- What would I do whether or not I got paid to do it?
- If I had a calling, what would it be?

Most of what I do in my work are things I would do whether or not I was paid to do them. I do them because I would miss them dearly if I didn't do them. This is how I can tell that my work is part of my calling. (It is not, however, the totality of it.) It is something I love to do. It enlivens me and brings me joy.

There was a time when, because of the intense nature of the work we do, Lura and I felt "burned out" and thought we wanted to change careers. At that point in my life, I was just starting to have, as hobbies, carpentry and remodeling. I thought I wanted to have a new career in the construction trades. As I tried to go in this direction, I noticed two things. The first is that absolutely *nothing* worked easily. There were no open doors, no serendipitous occurrences. There was no ease or sense of rightness about going in this direction. The second thing I noticed was how much I missed teaching and expressing the concepts I outline in this book.

As Lura and I took time to rest and nurture our family life, we realized that what was really needed was to learn more fully the lesson of including ourselves in what we taught, to release sacrifice more deeply, and to have more balance in our lives. As we did, things once again began to flow. I felt much more fulfilled, as if I was once again in touch with and expressing the wealth within me.

Our mission at Theophilus Divinity School is to support our students in discovering how they want to passionately participate in life, and to also support them in learning how to do this effectively as representatives of God. Those who complete the three years of school here and ask to be ordained understand that one of the definitions of the word "minister" is "representative." For example, France's Minister of Finance represents the government of France in this area. So, likewise, do each of us have an opportunity to represent Spirit in the area which speaks to us from our heart. As far as we are concerned, everyone has a calling, and one person's calling is no more or less holy than another's.

First Be, Then Do, Then Have

The way to be really successful in life is to decide who and what we want to be. The next step is to let what we want to be determine what we will do. The last is to let what we do determine what we will have, all the while working to release our inner blocks to prosperity and success.

It is an enormous sacrifice for us to do something we don't like to do for eight or ten hours each weekday so that the rest of our lives can be more enjoyable. This is being in survival mode. It means that we haven't yet learned that the universe wants to support us. We don't yet know that if we completely let go and relax, it will hold us up. Survival mode is still where most people in the world find themselves. The good news is that we don't have to stay there.

If you are doing what you are doing "for the money," it doesn't make you a bad person. It just means that you are underpaid, even if your annual income is in seven figures. It also means that you, like many of the rest of us, are learning some deep lessons on how to release sacrifice from your life.

This is obviously a fairly new concept, at least as far as the number of us who are now in a position to entertain it. When we look at our parents' lives, we see that most of them didn't live this way. For them, it was enough to work hard, to put food on the table, to provide for a family, to "make it through life without being a burden to anyone." Is there anything wrong with that? Of course not. But because many of us were born into a life in which survival was not an issue, we can stand on their shoulders and see that a better way of life is possible.

Letting Our Inner Magnificence Out

In that same generation, a prevailing psychological point of view was that we are basically bad, or sinful, or animalistic, and that we have to be controlled into being good. The good life, (or Heaven) was held out as a reward for being "good." In the last hundred years or so, some of us have begun to accept a "New Thought" (hence the birth of the New Thought Movement). This new thought, which is actually not new at all (but *is* much more widely accepted these days), is that we are not bad at all. We are inherently good. We are, in fact divine, created in the image and after the likeness of God. We don't need to be manipulated into doing good or loving people. It's what we do naturally as we learn to release our fear.

As Robert Browning said in his wonderful poem, "Paracelcus," ...and to *know* is to open *out* a way whence the imprisoned splendor may escape..." If we looked at the core of us, that's all we would find – splendor. In Emmett Fox's booklet, he says that our one sin (mistake) is suppression. I agree. Our job is to open out a way whence the imprisoned splendor may escape, to find a way to express ourselves which is tangible and beneficial to the community and the world. Our job, to echo Jesus, is to "let our light so shine that others may see our good works and glorify our Father in Heaven." (Mt. 5:16)

Learning to listen to our hearts is a way to practice listening to God in us. The word "desire" comes from a root word which means "of the father." The desires in our heart are God speaking to us from within saying what is possible for us.

Following Our Guidance Always Brings Us What We Want

This listening to our hearts is not a one-time occurrence. I first heard this voice in 1971, saying "you are going to be a minister." After I learned to open to it, there has been a steady stream of guidance since. When I wasn't open to hearing or following my guidance, I struggled, and my life became more difficult. When I was open to it, things worked, and my life became much easier.

For example, I was guided to move to Hawaii. The invitation was for me to come to Hawaii to supervise the renovation of the existing church and to start a new one. My then wife and I were moved there "all expenses paid". I didn't know it at the time, but the larger reason I was moving to Hawaii was so I could do my transformational work there. All I had to do, in order to get to the larger reason, was to say yes to my guidance. Hearing an inner voice (or sensing an inner feeling) and saying "yes" to it has turned out to be the theme for the rest of my life.

At the end of my Practitioner Training (the equivalent of the second year at our school in Minneapolis), I heard another voice. This one spoke through the theme song of a movie. (The Holy Spirit can speak through literally anything and anyone.) As I watched the movie **Flashdance**, and listened to the words, "Take your passion, and make it happen," I knew there was more for me to do than to remain as the minister of the church I had founded on Oahu. A T-shirt we had printed at that church said, "Live Your Dream." My passion was to teach, and my dream was to begin a school. So I resigned my position, even though I didn't know what I would do next. Each step of the way I was guided, first moving to Vancouver, Canada, so I could meet Lura, and then to Houston, Texas, where we could practice our skills, found yet another church, and get clearer on the kind of school we wanted to begin.

Following this, we took some time to rest, to integrate what we had learned, and to focus on our family life. Then we moved to Taos, New Mexico, once again because we were guided to do so. This was a further time of healing and purification for all of us, as well as a time to help a local church there get back on its feet. Then, a few months from the end of this final phase of preparation, I received a telephone call from my good friend, Howard Caesar, Senior Minister of one of the largest Unity churches. He called to say that he wanted to participate in a month-long residential program in Canada. He wanted to know if I would come to Houston and be the church's substitute Minister and Sunday speaker for that month.

The offer was for a wonderful salary, a car, all expenses, and the chance for a change of scenery. I knew that Lura could easily handle all the ministerial duties in Taos. The only down side I could see was that she and I would be apart for a month. But even that was made easier by the fact that Lura was already scheduled to lead a volunteer workshop at Howard's church about mid-month. I said I would love to come.

"It's Time to Start Your School"

In Houston, I stayed for part of the time with my oldest brother and his wife, and part of the time with our friends, Stav and Jerry Stefaniak, who do a similar work in Houston to what we offer in Minneapolis. The first two weeks at this church were just plain fun. Speaking to people from Houston has always been enjoyable for me, and in this case, I got to speak to 2,000 people at three services each Sunday.

On the second Sunday, I gave a talk about how to listen to and follow one's guidance. By Tuesday of the following week, my ears were so inflamed with an infection that I could hardly hear anything anyone said. By this time, many people at the Unity church had said things to me like, "We love to have you here. We can easily see you and Lura here in Houston, working with Howard at our church." I would guess that this happened twenty or more times. As I felt my ears aching, I thought, "I'm probably angry for hearing that our next step is to move back to Houston."

(Infections usually have something to do with anger, and Lura and I had lived in Houston some years before this. We loved the people, but we were not fond of the city's lifestyle.) My thoughts continued, "I probably just need to 'get real' and stop living some alternative lifestyle in Taos. We would be making a lot more money here than we ever could make there."

By Friday morning, my ears were so badly infected that they throbbed. I called in sick and asked my friend Stav Stefaniak to coach me in a Breath Integration Session. She said she'd be happy to do this and, as we began, asked me to tell her about my thoughts and feelings. I said that I thought the ear infections were the outpicturing of something I didn't want to hear, something I was angry about hearing. "What I think I'm angry about hearing," I continued, "is that it's probably time to stop this 'wandering in the wilderness' and move back to Houston. No doubt it's time to get a real job." Stav said, "Well, that's possible, Phil, but let's both try to tune into what the Holy Spirit has to say."

As I began to take in and release deep, oral breaths, it wasn't five minutes before I again heard a clear voice from within me say, "It's time to start your school of spiritual leadership." As soon as I heard it, I began to cry, and my ears immediately started to feel better. As I continued to breathe (and to cry), there was a feeling of gratitude for being so loved by God. By the end of the session there was hardly any pain at all. It was a nearly instantaneous healing!

By Saturday evening, there was barely even any sensitivity in my ears as I went to bed. Then, at 3 a.m., I awoke with pain in my right ear. I always get up early on Sunday mornings to work on my Sunday lesson, so I decided I might as well get up right then. I went out for coffee and began to work on my talk. By this time, my right ear was throbbing again, so I did what I often do when I want to be clearer on my guidance. I wrote a letter to God, and then I wrote one from God to me. I wrote, "Dear God, I think this pain in my right ear has something to do with my self-expression.

(The right side of the body often relates to our expressive side.) What do You want me to express in my talk this morning?" Then I did my best to tune into God consciousness and wrote, "Dear Phil, It's time to share publicly about your vision of a school for spiritual leadership." Then my anger *did* come to the surface. "Oh, fine," I thought. "This is a half-baked idea, at best. I have no idea about what this school even is, what is to be included, or where it is supposed to be located. And You want me to share this as my talk this morning?" I realized that even though I already had a very nice little talk ready to go, this clearly was my guidance. As soon as I said yes to it, my ear stopped hurting. By the time I did the three services that day, all the sensitivity in both ears was gone.

As I spoke that morning, I did share about my idea of a school for spiritual leadership and about what I had gone through that week. At the second service, (the largest one) I received a standing ovation at the end of the talk. As I stood there, enjoying the acknowledgment, I again felt grateful that I was able to feel my feelings, move through my resistance, receive God's love, and then extend it to others.

Responding to "Divine Discontent"

A life-long lesson for me, and for many others on a similar path, seems to be: *"Say yes to God, even though you don't feel ready, and even though you don't know how you will do it. God always has a plan, and you will almost always know only the next step. As you follow your guidance, you will continue to be success-ful and to prosper."* It was a few months after this experience that we decided to move to Minneapolis and to begin Theophilus Divinity School.

As I thought about how "at home" I feel in expressing my ministry, I remembered back to when I worked at Munsingwear as a Purchasing Agent. In those days, I did my best to fit in and to be a sensible businessman. I worked hard for the first few years, putting in a lot of overtime, because I thought that was what I needed to do to get ahead. Then, one night, as I was sitting in my office at 10 p.m., doing something which needed to be done to get the next season's line ready, I thought to myself, "I'm here at 10 p.m. so that a woman somewhere can buy a pair of designer underwear a day earlier than she otherwise could. What's wrong with this picture?"

There is, of course, nothing at all wrong with having one's passion be underwear – women's or men's. I am grateful that people are attracted to many, many fields in which I have no interest. The point is, with thoughts like these, this clearly wasn't *my* passion. Someone else would have been thinking, "What an opportunity. I get to be here doing what I love to do." But that wasn't my truth. I never did fit in when I tried to have a successful career in corporate America. I was a square peg in a round hole.

Someone coined a term I like: "divine discontent." One meaning of this term is that God is knocking at the door of our hearts whispering, *"This isn't what you came here to do. This is not how you wanted to express yourself."* When this happens, some of us have the thought, "I should just be happy here. There isn't a thing wrong with this job, vocation, profession, or business. I'll just try harder. I'll be sensible. I'll settle down."

Imagine how different the world would be if Jesus would have said to himself, "I simply have to let go of these grandiose ideas. I should be content to be a carpenter. My dad's a carpenter, and what's good enough for him is good enough for me. I need to get these Messiah thoughts out of my head." Imagine how different the world would be if Mother Teresa, Rosa Parks, Dr. Martin Luther King, or any one of a thousand other people we could name would have done the same. Then, imagine how much the world will be deprived if you don't give the gift you came here to give. Imagine, too, how much poorer your soul will be if you don't give it. As Abraham Maslow is said to have told those in some of his classes, "Which of you will be the next Marie Curie? The next Albert Schweitzer? And if not you, then who?"

There is a "Divine Plan" for each of our lives, including yours. There is a life for you which includes health, wealth, happiness, loving relationships, and perfect self-expression. I encourage you to have the intention of discovering that life, beginning with who and what you want to *be*. How do you go about it? By finding ways to simply become more conscious, more awake, more in touch with both your divinity and your humanity.

Tools to Help You Find and Live Your Vision

Here are some ways I have used. Some of these I have already mentioned (these probably can't be mentioned too often), and some of them are ones I haven't yet discussed:

1. Put your relationship with God first, and give your life to the Holy Spirit. The intention of this exercise is to become conscious of this *most real* part of your life. You might use the affirmation, "I now give my life to knowing God and to living my vision."

Some Bible experts say that the Old Testament could be summed up by saying that when the Israelites put God first in their lives, they prospered. When they stopped putting God first, they experienced want, famine, and war. So, too, it is in our lives. When we "Seek first the Kingdom of Heaven" (an experience of oneness with God), we prosper. When we don't, we experience inner famine and being at war with ourselves.

2. Practice paying attention to your heart. Practice opening your heart. Practice placing your attention at your heart center, and simply notice the sensations, feelings, and thoughts which come to you as you do. Practice listening to your heart's desires. Practice letting your heart lead the way. One way to do this is to do as I did when my ears were infected, and write a letter to God and one from God. This is because the place to find God within yourself is in your heart. If you have forgotten how to do this, it's easy, and the instructions are listed on page 20.

3. Do two writing exercises. The first is a list is titled, **"Something I deserve is ..."** (and then write as many things as come to you). When I wrote this list, it felt as if my heart just opened and jumped for joy when I saw, on paper, everything I claimed to deserve.

The second is a list called **"Twenty things I want to be,"** then **"twenty things I want to do,"** then **"twenty things I want to have."** This is a wonderful way to get clear on what you want to be, and to let that be the basis of your prosperity.

A Course In Miracles says that there will come a day when every one of us will experience success and prosperity in its fullest sense. It also says that this day could be a long, long way off. This is why Teachers of God are called for now. A Teacher of God, says *"The Course,"* is anyone who practices win/win in his or her life. It also says that each Teacher of God saves a thousand years, as the world measures time. So our assignment, should we choose to accept it, is a happy one. It is to be examples of people who become successful and prosperous by applying principles of love and oneness.

I ask you to join me in being committed to a conscious experience of oneness with God and oneness with all the people in the world. This is the essence of prosperity. As we, together, experience this oneness with Spirit, we will feel like we have come home, and our outer lives will increasingly reflect this real wealth which we find within ourselves.

Dear God, thank you for showing me how to know my oneness with you, my oneness with all my neighbors, my love for the earth, and my love for all my creations. Amen.

Appendix A

Prosperity Affirmations

Affirmations to Support You in Prospering and Creating the Life You Deserve

1. God in me _____ (always include your first name) is the unlimited Source of everything I want, including (money, love, time, etc.).
2. No matter how my needs and desires are met, I know that everything comes from God in me.
3. I am now open to receive all forms of God's love, including money.
4. God in me is the unlimited Source of everything I want, and God always succeeds.
5. The more I know God in me as my one Source, the more prosperous and peaceful I become.
6. I am now free to know what I want, to ask for what I want, and to have what I want.
7. God in me loves it when I have enough money to live my vision.
8. The divine plan that God in me has for my life is now manifesting, and I see it.
9. My wealth contributes to my happiness, and my happiness contributes to my wealth.
10. My wealth contributes to my freedom, and my freedom contributes to my wealth.

11. I always receive lots of money for doing what I love to do, because I deserve it.
12. I always have enough time, energy, wisdom, and money to accomplish all my desires.
13. The more I surrender to my innocence, the more prosperous I become.
14. I am rich in God. The richer I feel in God's qualities, the richer my life becomes.
15. The more I surrender to and express the love in me, the more prosperous I become.
16. I always look for the divine in myself and everyone else, so my life always reflects it.
17. I now fully accept my power of creation, and my life becomes ever richer and fuller.
18. I now open to and express my connection with God, so my life becomes ever wealthier.
19. I deserve to have an intimate relationship with God in me, and I now have one.
20. I always do what I enjoy, and I always enjoy what I do.
21. My activities always create prosperity for me and everyone else.
22. I always love myself and am filled with confidence, so my life gets ever richer.
23. I deserve to be prosperous and to have what I want.
24. I have great worth just for being here and being myself.
25. Prosperity and happiness are natural for me as a child of God.
26. I easily and joyously express all my creative potential.
27. I am a master of money. It serves my happiness and my spiritual growth.
28. I always use money to more fully express my spirituality in the world.
29. There is an abundance for everyone, including me, and I claim it now.

30. The world is an abundant, wonderful place to be, and I love to be here.
31. My prosperity prospers others, and their prosperity prospers me.
32. I am now open to freely give and freely receive money.
33. An abundance of everything I want is available from God, and I can have it.
34. I am now willing to receive lots of love and money, even if it brings up my helpless feelings.
35. I am now willing to receive lots of love and money, even if it brings up (fear, anger, guilt).
36. My worth is established by God, so I am worth a fortune.
37. I enjoy making lots of money. Making lots of money is safe, fun, and easy.
38. I always receive money and love with gratitude and innocence.
39. Every part of me is ready, willing, and able to have lots of (love, money, time) now.
40. Money is a wonderful tool. I use it to create possibilities for myself and everyone in my life.
41. I know who I am when I am successful.
42. I feel comfortable and at home in the presence of successful people.
43. The universe is a friendly place and willingly provides all I need to be successful.
44. My wealth constantly builds, whether I am working, playing, resting, or sleeping.
45. My connection with Universal Mind is an unlimited source of money-making ideas, and I now open to it.
46. A part of every dollar I make is mine to keep, so I do.
47. I always make all the money I want doing what I love to do.
48. I trust myself to manage money wisely and responsibly.
49. I now allow myself to have as much money as I want.
50. I am the rich child of a loving inner Parent.

51. The more I prosper and have what I want, the more everyone wins.
52. The more others prosper and have what they want, the more I win.
53. As I see with the eyes of Christ, I see God's abundance everywhere, including in me.
54. I now completely open my heart, so I can have all the love and money I want.
55. I love God, and God loves me. I love money, and money loves me.
56. I always say yes to God in me, and God shows me how to live my vision, one step at a time.
57. I am committed to loving myself and having the life I want.
58. I am now free to commit to my happiness and well-being.
59. I am cause of every experience I have.
60. Everything I want is already within me, and I see it.
61. Everything that seems to happen to me is my idea, including _____.
62. I now embrace all my creations so I can receive the gift I want from each one.
63. I now fully accept and express my power of creation.
64. I give myself permission to have more love, money, and success than my parents (do/did).
65. I now embrace all my emotions, especially _____.
66. I now forgive everyone who I thought harmed me.
67. I now forgive myself for every time I thought I harmed anyone.
68. I now surrender to my purpose, which is to experience oneness with God and to live my vision.
69. Everything I do prospers me and everyone in my life.
70. I deserve to ask for and hear God's guidance every day.
71. I now surrender to and express my inner wealth, so my life becomes ever richer.
72. The more I give to others, the more I have. The more others give to me, the more they have.

Appendix B

How to Feel and Express Angry Feelings

Note: This is from an article written by the Reverend Lisa Bergerud. Lisa wrote a paper on how to express anger when she was a third-year student at Theophilus Divinity School. We now use this article as a handout. My thanks to her for giving me permission to include part of it in this book.

- Are you frequently late?
- Do you lose your temper over insignificant things?
- Do you frequently feel annoyed, irritated, or grouchy?
- Do you "forget" to keep agreements?
- Do you judge people for openly expressing anger?
- Do you withhold love, affection, sex, or money from others?
- Do you give people the silent treatment?
- Are you sarcastic?
- Do you have lots of critical thoughts of others?
- Are you often depressed?

If you see yourself in one or more of these questions, you are almost certainly suppressing your anger. In other words, you are expressing your anger in inappropriate ways – ways which can hurt you, hurt others, and hurt your relationships. Here, then, are some techniques which can support you in expressing anger in appropriate ways:

1. Simply notice you're feeling angry. To the best of your ability, feel it, be with it in your body, and *breathe*.

2. If you are with the person who is triggering your angry feelings, say, as responsible as you can, "I felt angry when you _____," rather than, "You made me angry when you _____." Then excuse yourself and let yourself have a good scream or "temper tantrum."

3. Let yourself scream or yell angry words into a pillow or a towel (100% cotton works far better than artificial fibers). Give yourself the opportunity to express (in uncensored language) whatever it is you'd most like to say in the moment. Simply let it out of your body.

4. Have a temper tantrum. Most of us were stopped from having tantrums when we were children, so now is the time to really give it to ourselves. Tantrums can look like lying on your bed, kicking your legs, and flailing your arms while screaming into a pillow. You can do this either on your back or on your stomach. If you are lying on your back, hold your legs fairly straight and "scissor" them up and down. When lying on your stomach, make fists and beat the bed with them while you yell into the pillow.

5. Another way to have a temper tantrum is to hit your bed with a tennis or racquetball racket.

6. Yet another way to express angry feelings is to be on your feet and stomp around. The object is to simply move the energy through and out of your body, rather than to hold onto it

7. Still another way to work with anger is to buy a heavy bag, hit it with a baseball bat, and really let yourself get into it. This, by the way, is one of the most responsible and safest ways to express anger. It is much better to express anger this way than

to have it "leak out" while you are in your car (road rage), or in a fight with a loved one, or by severely disciplining your children or animals. If you're unsure of how to have a tantrum, look for a three-year-old who is upset (the next time you are in the grocery store) and take notes – they're experts.

8. Be willing to know that whenever you are upset you are in the past. Ask yourself, "Who or what does this remind me of?" See if you can find the source of the original upset, and then let yourself continue screaming and/or having a tantrum as if you were a child. Since childhood anger is often so buried, it is often necessary to give yourself some time at the start of your session to "project" your angry feelings onto the current people who are triggering them. Ultimately, though, the object is to discover what is being activated from the past and give your inner child time *now* to do what he or she couldn't do *then*. This is a way of loving and honoring your inner child. It is important to understand that you will never release or resolve your angry feelings by thinking or yelling about current-day situations. The reason they are here is that you are trying to resolve issues from the past.

9. Be willing to know that anger is just a feeling. It is not who you are. You are a person having angry feelings, not an "angry person," and the feeling is temporary. The sooner you let yourself feel and express it, the sooner it will shift and pass.

10. Schedule a Breath Integration (or Rebirthing) Session. (See Appendix D.) A Breath Integration Session is a completely supportive and safe environment to feel and express your anger and to learn how to be more responsible with it. You will also receive support in addressing the underlying causes of it. (Note: All Theophilus-trained Breath Integration Practitioners have learned to face, feel, and express their anger in appropriate ways. They are dedicated to creating a safe environment for this important work. If you are choosing a Re-

birther to work with, make sure you find one who has faced, felt, and become comfortable expressing his or her own angry feelings.)

Ultimately, whoever (or whatever) is "making you angry" is your idea and your creation. This is happening because there is some part of you that, until now, you have been unconscious of, and because you are trying to awaken to it. You will find that as you commit ·to feeling and expressing your angry feelings in appropriate ways, you will have fewer and fewer people in your life who reflect your own anger. You will also have fewer situations in your life which trigger your anger.

Appendix C

How to Make a Treasure Map

Note: The following is a handout at our school. It was originally an article written by three members of the school's third-year class. I would like to thank The Reverends Lisa Bergerud, Janet Rasmussen, and JoAnne Sax for their permission to include it in this book.

A treasure map is a pictured prayer or visual affirmation. It is a method of consciously claiming your goals and desires in the form of a collage of images and words. Making a treasure map is a way to focus the power of your mind and heart on what you want to create. It is an outward act of "placing an order" to the universe, so the universe can respond and fulfill it. Imagine going into a restaurant and wanting to get served – but not placing an order. You may be waiting a long time to receive your food. It is much the same way with your life. If you don't ask for what you want in your life, it is far less likely that you'll receive it. Creating a treasure map is a perfect way to claim what you really want to receive and to take direct responsibility for co-creating it with God.

Making a treasure map works with both your conscious and sub-conscious mind. Every time you look at your map you are consciously reminding yourself of your goals and desires, as well as sub-consciously imprinting, time and time again, that this is actually attainable. Looking at your treasure map keeps you focused and on track by constantly affirming the direction you are heading.

Making a treasure map is a physical demonstration of claiming your intentions. It is a simple and fun process and can be easily completed in an afternoon. To begin with, you will need the following:

SUPPLIES

- **Poster board** (we recommend 22" x 28" – the largest size normally stocked at discount, office supply, and art supply stores)
- **Glue sticks**
- **Scissors**
- **Magazines, catalogs, brochures** (ones which reflect your interests)
- **A picture of yourself** (that you find pleasing and want to look at)

PREPARATION

1. Write a purpose and goals for your treasure map.

Get clear on how you want your life to improve. Ask yourself, "What is the one area of my life I would most like to improve?" Is it career? Relationships? Health? Finances? Leisure? Hobbies/ travel? Spirituality? Creative expression? (We suggest you begin with only one of these areas as the focus for your first treasure map. Once you become more familiar with the process, you can incorporate a variety of areas on future treasure maps.)

2. Gather visual images, words, phrases, and numbers that will appear on your map.

Collect various magazines, catalogs, and brochures that have images, words, and phrases that represent what you want to have in your life. Allow yourself some time to page through and collect the images and words that "speak" to you about what you are claiming.

For instance, if your treasure map focuses on improving your finances, you can find pictures of paper money, coins, numbers, wealthy people, and any material objects like cars and homes that represent the financial success you are claiming.

If you want a new primary relationship, find pictures of people who are enjoying each other's company or are in some way demonstrating what you want. Look for words and phrases that describe your ideal relationship (e.g. loving, empowering, happiness, partnership, intimacy, joy, etc.). As you find the images and words that apply to your treasure map, cut them out and place them in a pile. Gather all of them. You will sort them out later.

3. Find a picture of yourself.

You will place this photograph in the center of your treasure map. This is a way for you to visually affirm that what you are claiming is for you. It is a way of literally seeing yourself surrounded by and receiving what you are claiming. It is important that you place a photo of yourself that you enjoy looking at, since you will be connecting with your treasure map daily. However, if you do not like *any* photo of yourself, do not let that stop you from making a treasure map. Simply use the one you dislike the least, and practice loving yourself as you look at your picture.

4. Find a picture that represents God.

This could be a picture of anything from a sunset to a mountain range or other nature scene to a picture of Jesus or the Buddha. Whatever speaks to you of God. This symbol of God will go at the top of your treasure map as a reminder that your relationship with God comes first and that everything you receive in your life comes from God in you.

In creating this treasure map you are consciously asking God in you for support in manifesting your specific desires. One of the beauties of a treasure map is that *you* needn't determine how you will receive your goals. You just need to trust God, as your one and only unlimited Source, to provide.

5. Include a "cosmic clause" affirmation.

At the bottom of your treasure map, write (or print out from your computer) an affirmation like *"This or something better now manifests easily, in ways which serve the highest good of all concerned."* If you like, you can add a specific statement related to your goal at the beginning of the general affirmation, such as *"I _____ (your name) now easily and gratefully receive my perfect mate. This or something better..."* The affirmation should be stated in present tense. By doing this, you acknowledge that your goal has already been achieved. You also acknowledge that you are asking for the *essence* of this desire and are not attached to receiving it in any certain form. God in you knows the form which will most support you (and everyone else).

ASSEMBLY

1. Begin by gluing the photograph of yourself in the center of the poster board. This represents the idea that not only do these desires exist, they exist *in your experience*.

2. Place the representation of your Source above your picture. This reminds you that your first and foremost goal is to nurture your relationship with God in you as the one Source of everything you want.

3. Before gluing, arrange your pictures, words, and phrases on the poster board. Move them around to get a sense of where you want them to be placed. Play with it, and have fun!

4. Glue or write your "cosmic clause" (centered) at the bottom of the map.

5. Glue your images and words into place.

6. Hang your treasure map in a place where you can effortlessly view it every day. For example, hang it on your bedroom wall or door, or place it on the bathroom wall opposite the toilet. Spend a few seconds or minutes each day looking at your treasure map, and watch as you manifest your heart's desires!

When you finish your treasure map, you will have completed a powerful process that will support you in enhancing your sense of spiritual, physical, and emotional fulfillment in your life. You will have done this by more deeply claiming your relationship with God in you and by directly asking God for one of your desires. Remind yourself how safe it is to actually have what you want. Knowing, asking for, and receiving what you want might be unfamiliar at times, but it is your inherent birthright.

When your map is finished, congratulate yourself on committing this much to having what you want in your life. You deserve it, simply by being a child of God. And enjoy yourself as you watch miracles occur!

Appendix D

Breath Integration Sessions

How Breath Integration Sessions Can Support You

A series of Breath Integration or Rebirthing Sessions with a qualified Practitioner or Rebirther is a powerful, yet gentle, tool with which to support your transformation on all levels – spiritual, mental, emotional, and physical. Most of us only breathe a fraction of our capacity, and we hold our breath when we experience something fearful. Among the effects of this are that thinking becomes more difficult, and emotion is suppressed.

Your breath is your physical connection to life energy itself, so even the cells of your body are rejuvenated as you breathe deeply. With deep breathing, you will feel healthier and more relaxed, and you will also feel more alive than you may have thought was possible. Fuller, freer breathing literally results in a fuller freer life.

The more you can bring to light and learn to love all aspects of yourself, the more rapidly you will see positive changes in your life. The following are some of the parts of yourself you can more fully open to, accept, and embrace through doing this kind of breathwork.

- **Your inner child and your inner adolescent.** These still live in you. Without you knowing it, they will be making your major decisions for you until you can accept and love (reintegrate) them.

- **Your emotions.** These include the love, joy, and enthusiasm in you. They also include the anger, sadness, fear, and guilt in you which have acted as unconscious barriers to creating the kind of life you want.
- **Your subconscious thoughts**, including the decisions you made at an early age which are still creating unwanted results in your life.
- **Your true desires**, personal vision, and ways you want to passionately participate in life.
- **Your oneness with God**, including your intuition, your sense of aliveness, your power of creation, and your innocence.
- **Your oneness with the people in your life.**

Describing a Breath Integration Session

A private Breath Integration (or Rebirthing) Session lasts about two hours. It includes a consultation, a half-hour to an hour of a kind of deep oral breathing, and a time of completion. A group Breath Integration Session may last a longer time, to give everyone a chance to share and receive support.

In these sessions, you will experience breathing deeply and fully, both inhaling and exhaling through your mouth. This type of oral breathing is an ancient Yogic technique. It is designed to support you in awakening to yourself and in becoming more conscious, both of your divinity and of your humanity. It is very much like peeling away layers of an onion, the core of the onion being your divine self.

The main aspects to this breathing method are: breathing both in and out through your mouth; filling your lungs as completely as possible on each inhale; relaxing as much as possible on each exhale, and keeping your breaths "connected." This means beginning another exhale as soon as you reach the "top" of your inhale, and beginning another inhale as soon as you reach the "bottom" of your exhale.

During the half-hour to hour of this breathing practice, the job of your Breath Coach or Rebirther is to support you in breathing as described above. It is also to provide you with an environment of safety and unconditional love, and to "hold the consciousness" on knowing that God in you is in charge of your experience. The Breath Coach will help you move through any fears which arise in you. He or she will also help you open to, embrace, and love whatever aspect of yourself is coming to the surface. In other words, a Breath Integration Session is fundamentally non-directed. The focus is on what presents itself as you practice this deep breathing. As a result, you feel *more* in charge of your own life, rather than like you have given control of it to another person.

Breath Integration Sessions are also a form of "surrender practice." That is, they are a way to practice surrendering to God in you and to the aspects of God which are in everyone – Aliveness, Love, Wisdom, and true Power. They are also a way to practice receiving. As you take in deep, full breaths (life energy, prana) and relax on the exhale (practice letting go rather than either forcing the air out or holding on and letting a little out at a time), it is as if an imprint is made on the very cells of your body, the memory of which supports you long after the session has ended.

About Your Breath Practitioner or Rebirther

The mental/emotional/spiritual environment created by the consciousness of the counselor is immensely important. People who work with a Theophilus-trained Breath Practitioner regularly tell us that these are some of the most profound experiences they have ever had. We believe that one reason for this is the degree of safety and the amount of love we can let flow through us. This, in turn, is the result of the work we have done on ourselves – the degree to which we have resolved our own inner conflicts and faced our own fears. We think it is also because we have learned to have a high level of trust in God to guide us in each session we coach. Another asset we bring to each session is our love. Each of us who has decided to be a Breath Integration Practitioner is doing so because of how much we have received from these sessions, and because we want to extend to others what we have received.

If you decide to work with a Rebirther, be sure to apply the same standards you would for any counseling session you want to try. How do you feel about him or her? What kind of background and/or training does she or he have? Do you feel safe with this person? Does he or she seem competent? Loving? Comfortable with her or his own emotions and issues?

Are Breath Integration Sessions For You?

No one *needs* a Breath Integration or Rebirthing Session. For that matter, no one needs a workshop, book, or class on spiritual principles. These are devices designed to both save time and to result in having an easier time learning the lessons of life. Eventually, life itself would teach us everything there is to know about ourselves. However, "eventually" can be a very long time, and "life itself" is not necessarily a gentle teacher.

Who these sessions *are* for are certain people who, in some way, come into contact with this tool. These people feel an inner pull or hear an inner voice or thought saying, "Try this." For many of us, this voice was the voice of the Holy Spirit saying, *"This is the answer to your prayer about how to have your spiritual path be easier and more direct."*

How Do You Find a Practitioner or Rebirther?

At this time, I am aware of Breath Integration Practitioners only in a few cities. It will be much easier to find a Rebirther. One place to look for one is in your city's "alternative" newspapers (recovery, holistic healing, New Age, etc.).

If you are interested in trying a Breath Integration Session and immersing yourself in these teachings for a week, our school currently offers a weeklong workshop in late summer each year. You can call Theophilus Divinity School at (612) 724-4916 or visit our website at **www.tdsonline.org** for the current schedule.

Appendix E

Symptoms of Suppressed Emotional Pain

Note: The following list is intended only as a guide to support you in becoming more conscious of your emotional life. For a more specific correlation with a particular physical illness or condition, I suggest you consult Louise Hay's book You Can Heal Your Life.

General Symptoms of Suppressed Emotions

- Being depressed
- Being "numb" or not knowing how you feel most of the time
- Having little success with such techniques as affirmations or visualization
- Living "not to lose" instead of living to win
- Having the thought that the best it gets is when you are free of pain
- Living in "crisis management"
- Trying to get the people in your presence to stop expressing their feelings (and/or judging them for "being so emotional")
- Not remembering large segments of your childhood
- Being addicted to food, drugs, sex, television, sleep, work, etc.
- Having little or no physical sensation in your body

- Being aware that you are constantly acting – having little spontaneity
- Being afraid of receiving too much love, money, support, or affection
- Being moody
- When you talk to others, having those around you be frequently confused, angry, sleepy, or not understand you (the 60% or your communication which is non-verbal contradicts what you say)
- Being frequently "out of your body," living "in your head," or not "being fully present" most of the time
- Having frequent illnesses, accidents, or other painful things "happen" to you

Symptoms of Suppressed Anger

- Frequently being late
- Judging people for openly expressing anger
- Withholding love, affection, sex, or money from others
- Giving someone the "silent treatment"
- "Forgetting" to keep agreements (forgetting is a choice)
- Not letting others love you or win with you
- Losing your temper over insignificant things
- Being sarcastic
- Frequently criticizing others or having critical thoughts
- Failing – in school, your career, your relationships
- Succeeding to get even (if someone told you that you'd never amount to anything)
- Having others be frequently angry at you
- Yelling at or otherwise abusing children or pets
- Having lots of angry people in your life
- Having illnesses with fevers
- Feeling controlled by others, life, or God
- Feeling depressed a lot, regularly having "the blahs"
- Having violent fantasies or dreams

- Grinding your teeth in your sleep, or having a clenched jaw

Symptoms of Suppressed Extreme Anger

- Raping, abusing, or otherwise violently treating people (including children) and/or animals
- Being raped or otherwise violently treated
- Breaking things when you lose your temper
- Committing suicide

Symptoms of Suppressed Guilt

- Hurting yourself
- Wanting to be punished so you will feel better
- Procrastinating (so you can continue to feel guilty)
- Believing that people (including children) need to be punished
- Thinking you have to keep secrets from those closest to you
- Not keeping your agreements and not communicating or making new ones
- Having a feeling of "waiting for the other shoe to drop"
- Sabotaging yourself when you are about to receive something you want, or when you have just received it
- Feeling "special" or different from other people
- Thinking "If people really knew me, they wouldn't like me"
- A feeling of low self-esteem, a belief that you don't deserve love, ease, joy, or success
- Being judgmental – disowning your "self-attack" thoughts and projecting them onto others
- Having bill collectors calling or writing you
- Getting traffic or parking tickets
- Having things stolen from you (having an unconscious belief that you are stealing from life)
- Being a perfectionist
- Believing that there is something wrong with you, or that there is something missing in you

- Comparing yourself to others, regularly feeling better than or less than others

Symptoms of Suppressed Fear

- Attempting to be in control – of your emotions, of others, of life, of the future, of God
- Being shy, avoiding people
- Being over-talkative, being uncomfortable with silence
- Frequently judging others or yourself
- Laughing when something isn't funny to you
- Being attracted to scary movies
- Being obsessed with body building, martial arts, self-defense
- Nervous habits
- Frequent worrying or free-floating anxiety, anxiety "attacks"
- Constipation or diarrhea
- Tightness in your chest

Symptoms of Suppressed Sadness

- A feeling of heaviness in your chest
- Losing things you value
- Being attracted to sad movies, melancholy songs
- Having people leave you
- Having things you love be taken away from you
- Having pets or plants die
- Telling yourself you don't really care about the people or things in your life
- Being obsessed with protecting yourself from loss
- Physical symptoms such as congestion, excess of phlegm (crying on the inside) or diabetes
- Holding onto the past, being unwilling to release what isn't working
- Becoming upset when in the presence of someone who is crying (especially a baby)

Affirmations to Support You in Becoming Conscious of and Appropriately Expressing Your Emotions

1 I _____ now see that all my feelings are important.

2 All my emotions are acceptable to me _____, especially _____(name of the emotion you most judge)

3 I _____ give my relationship with my emotions to the Holy Spirit.

4 I _____ give my relationship with _____(name of the emotion you hate or are afraid of) to the Holy Spirit.

5 I _____ now give myself permission to feel, express, and release my emotional pain.

6 I _____ no longer need my parents' permission to express my feelings, because I have my own.

7 I _____ love myself for having feelings, especially _____ (name of emotion you most judge or hate).

8 It is easy, safe, and rewarding for me _____ to express all my feelings, especially _____.

9 I _____ now value my emotional life so much that I always know how I feel.

Other Products Available from Theophilus Publishing:

Cassette Tape Albums:

Power Packed Prosperity Principles. Eight cassette tapes, re-corded at a series of lectures, with the same life-changing message as this book – how to experience the prosperity and abundance you deserve, beginning on the inside.

The Bible as a Tool of Transformation. A three-cassette (six-class) series on how to "make friends with the Bible" and let it support you in transforming your life. This personal transformation, or how to live in the Kingdom of Heaven, was the primary teaching of Jesus Christ.

A Guide to "A Course In Miracles". Four cassette tapes covering eight classes led by Phil and Lura Smedstad on the principles and practices of *A Course In Miracles*. In these classes, the Smedstads share their unique perspective as teachers of both emotional purification and spiritual principles.

The Prayer of Transformation. This is an eighteen page booklet on a small-group prayer program called the Prayer of Transformation and a three-cassette tape album. The tapes explain each step of the prayer as well as how to start and maintain a group. Many have called this the most powerful prayer program they've ever seen. It teaches the principles of personal transformation and helps participants learn that "all miracles happen within them."

Other Products:

Let Spirit Lead Us. This 165-page book is a manual and guide for leaders of volunteer organizations. Written by Lura Smedstad, it teaches how to have all volunteer activities support both the spiritual growth of the volunteer and the well-being of the organization. The book includes a section on the steps the Smedstads took as they founded a new church based on this system.

The "My Next Step" Cards. This deck is a set of 100 action steps to support its user in transforming his or her life from fear-based to love-filled. Practical, powerful, and direct, these cards are a self-directed course in personal and spiritual growth. Having them is like having a spiritual coach in your pocket.

The "My Next Step" CD. This is the same self-directed course in personal transformation as the above cards, in a format which can be easily loaded onto your PC. Each time you turn on your computer (or click on the *My Next Step* icon), it will show you your next step in transforming your life.

How Tithing Prospers You. This is a 16 page booklet by Phil Smedstad. Several New Thought ministers have said that this approach to tithing makes the most sense of any they've read. Over 100 New Thought churches and groups have used this booklet as a mailer or a handout.

For information on current prices of these products and how to order them, please call Theophilus Divinity School at 1-866-300-4916 or visit our website at www.tdsonline.org.

About the Author

The Reverend Phillip Smedstad is the co-founder of Theophilus Divinity School in Minneapolis, Minnesota. He and his wife, Lura, founded this three-year course in personal ministry in 1993. Phil is the author of the **My Next Step** cards, an inner-directed course in personal transformation, and of the **My Next Step** CD (the same course available for use on personal computers). He also wrote **How Tithing Prospers You**, a booklet which has been used as a handout at over a hundred Unity and Religious Science churches. In addition, Phil has produced a number of cassette tape albums, including **Making Friends With the Bible** (the Bible as a tool for personal transformation), **A Guide to A Course In Miracles**, and **Power Packed Prosperity Principles**.

In his previous career as a Unity minister, Phil was the leader of churches in Florida, Hawaii, Texas, and New Mexico. Two of these churches are ones he founded. Phil graduated from Unity's ministerial school in 1976.